CONCILIUM

CONCILIUM
ADVISORY COMMITTEE

Gregory Baum	Montreal, QC Canada
José Oscar Beozzo	São Paulo, SP Brazil
Wim Beuken	Louvain Belgium
Leonardo Boff	Petrópolis, RJ Brazil
John Coleman	Los Angeles, CA USA
Christian Duquoc	Lyon France
Virgil Elizondo	San Antonio, TX USA
Claude Geffré	Paris France
Norbert Greinacher	Tübingen Germany
Gustavo Gutiérrez	Lima Peru
Hermann Häring	Tübingen Germany
Werner G. Jeanrond	Glasgow Scotland
Jean-Pierre Jossua	Paris France
Maureen Junker-Kenny	Dublin Ireland
François Kabasele Lumbala	Kinshasa Dem. Rep. of Congo
Nicholas Lash	Cambridge England
Mary-John Mananzan	Manila Philippines
Alberto Melloni	Reggio Emilia Italy
Norbert Mette	Münster Germany
Dietmar Mieth	Tübingen Germany
Jürgen Moltmann	Tübingen Germany
Teresa Okure	Port Harcourt Nigeria
Aloysius Pieris	Kelaniya, Colombo Sri Lanka
David Power	Washington, D.C. USA
Giuseppe Ruggieri	Catania Italy
Paul Schotsmans	Louvain Belgium
Janet Martin Soskice	Cambridge England
Elsa Tamez	San José Costa Rica
Christoph Theobald	Paris France
David Tracy	Chicago, IL USA
Marciano Vidal	Madrid Spain
Ellen van Wolde	Tilburg Holland

CONCILIUM 2013/5

REFORM OF THE ROMAN CURIA

Edited by

Luiz Carlos Susin, Silvia Scatena
& Susan Ross

SCM Press · London

Published in 2013 by SCM Press, 3rd Floor, Invicta House, 108-114 Golden Lane, London EC1Y 0TG.

SCM Press is an imprint of Hymns Ancient & Modern Ltd (a registered charity) 13A Hellesdon Park Road, Norwich NR6 5DR, UK

Copyright © International Association of Conciliar Theology, Madras (India)

www.concilium.in

English translations copyright © 2013 Hymns Ancient & Modern Ltd.

All rights reserved. No part of this publication may be reproduced, stored in a retrieval system, or transmitted, in any form or by any means, electronic, mechanical, photocopying or otherwise, without the prior written permission of the Board of Directors of Concilium.

ISBN 9780334031260

Printed in the UK by
CPI Antony Rowe, Chippenham, Wiltshire

Contents

Preface: Why this Special Issue   7

Editorial: Reform of the Roman Curia   9

Part One: Lessons from History

Reform of the Roman Curia through History   15
NORMAN TANNER SJ

Reform of the Roman Curia at and after Vatican II   25
MASSIMO FAGGIOLI

Part Two: The Canonical and Institutional Level

Senatus Communionis: A Senate of Communion   35
ALBERTO MELLONI

Cognitive Dissonance?   51
GERARD MANNION

Roman Primacy, Communion between Churches, and Communion
between Bishops   63
HERVÉ LEGRAND OP

Women in the Lead: Even in the Roman Curia   78
SABINE DEMEL

From a Seventeenth-century Court to a Modern Service   88
THOMAS J. REESE SJ

Renewal and Clarity in the Government of the Church　　97
CELSO QUEIROZ OSB

Part Three: Spiritual, Pastoral and Ecumenical Dimensions

Ecumenical Implications of Reforming the Curia　　108
WALTER ALTMANN

Spiritual and Pastoral Guidelines for a Reform of the Curia　　117
PETER HÜNERMANN

Part Four: Theological Forum

Rio World Youth Day and Evangelization　　131
LÚCIA PEDROSA-PÁDUA

European Theologians Meet at Brixen, Italy　　137
THIERRY-MARIE COURAU OP

CONTRIBUTORS　　148

Preface: Why this Special Issue

FELIX WILFRED

Exactly one month after his election, on 13 April 2013, Pope Francis announced his intention to carry out a serious reform of the Roman Curia by appointing a committee of eight cardinals from different parts of the world. The editorial board of the international theological review *Concilium*, which met in Montreal in May 2013, saw this proposal as a great sign of renewal for the Church, and an opportunity to put into effect the spirit of the Council and some of its central teachings on the People of God, the collegiality of bishops, sharing responsibility, and the participation of the laity in the mission and governance of the Church. The post-conciliar reforms of the Curia remained, unfortunately, at the surface level, and did not address some of the deeper and most important issues in the light of these teachings. Moreover, these teachings, it would seem, were held at bay lest the Curia's hold on power as the central organ in the governance of the Church should be threatened, something exemplified in the way synods were conducted, the bishops' conferences were dealt with, and the role of the laity was obscured. In sum, in spite of the great ecclesiological vision and openings of the Council, and its explicit call and directives for the reform of the Roman Curia, there was the feeling of a backward movement to the past and to business as usual.

The review *Concilium* understands its mission as that of keeping the torch of Vatican II burning through its theological service to the entire Church. This sense of mission prompted the members of the editorial board to seize the opportunity and help the Church and Pope Francis to accomplish the unfinished task of reforming the Roman Curia. It was decided to make a study of the question of reform from various perspectives: historical, theological, ecclesiological, canonical and pastoral. Normally, 18 months is the time-line for the preparation of any issue of *Concilium*. However, in the case of the reform of the Roman Curia, *Concilium* felt a sense of urgency about ensuring that its contribution would appear without delay,

Preface

and decided to prepare this special issue as *Concilium* 5/2013. It meant postponing the issue on 'Orthodoxy' to 2014. The greatest difficulty, as can be imagined, was to find authors for this special issue, who would be able to write and deliver their articles promptly without compromising quality. We were fortunate to find some of the most outstanding scholars willing to contribute essays at short notice on various questions making up this issue. I appreciate their dedication and thank them for their hard work and valuable contributions.

Without the cooperation and unstinting support of the colleagues of *Concilium*, this issue would not have seen the light of day. Contacting the writers and editing this special issue was entrusted to three colleagues: Luiz Carlos Susin, Susan Ross and Silvia Scatena. They have worked together to plan the issue, its content and orientation. I wish to express my sincere thanks for the work they have accomplished. I would like to single out the dedicated efforts of Luiz Carlos Susin, who played the rôle of convener for the preparation of the issue. For me and for the Secretariat of *Concilium*, it was a great pleasure to dialogue with him and accompany him in the final editing of the manuscripts. Our sincere thanks go to all our six language edition publishers for their flexibility in accommodating this special issue, translating and preparing articles, and bringing out the issue in record time. Arokia Mary Anthony Das (Nirmal), the managing secretary of *Concilium*, played a crucial rôle in coordinating the preparation of this issue with her characteristic dedication, patience and amazing concentration. I wish to thank her very warmly for her service.

The way Roman Curia operates, the decisions it takes and the choices it makes affect the Church at all levels, and therefore its reform is a concern of all believers. By bringing out this special issue, *Concilium* invites its readers to be involved actively in this reform process. For this purpose, *Concilium* has also taken the initiative of organizing a presentation of this issue in Rome in late 2013, in cooperation with the Italian publisher Queriniana. It is the hope of *Concilium* that the reflections that make up this issue will benefit the People of God and encourage them to play an active role in the reform process, in keeping with the spirit and teachings of Vatican II.

Felix Wilfred
President, Concilium

Editorial
Reform of the Roman Curia

2013 was a year marked by events that will have incalculable consequences for the life of the Catholic Church, especially when considered in relation to its centre in Rome.

First, there was Benedict XVI's resignation, an ecclesial act unequalled in modern times. With this move, for which he will certainly go down in history, Benedict XVI catapulted the papacy into a new dimension for the modern age, as Paul VI had done previously with regard to the bishops, because his historic act of resignation, which distinguished between the office and its holder, abandoned the sacral quality that previously united person and mission ontologically. The Petrine ministry can now display more sustainably what it really is, that is, a service, a ministry devoted to the universal communion of the Church. Once an individual ceases to be able to perform this important service and mission, that person gives it up, of his or her own free will, so that someone else can carry it out more adequately and effectively. This message came across loud and clear in the list of reasons Benedict XVI, of his own free will, gave in his act of resignation.

Second, we had the election of Jorge Mario, Archbishop of Buenos Aires, as Bishop of Rome and, consequently, the new Pope. In taking to the see of Rome his pastoral life-style, a life-style that quickly became famous in countless surprising and telling details, Pope Francis began his ministry by acting on the suggestions he had received from Benedict XVI and the college of cardinals that elected him. These suggestions were and are about reform, about prioritizing the need to bring about changes in the Church's government. At the end of his pontificate, Benedict XVI referred repeatedly to the urgent need to renew the church community, and stressed the fact that any such renewal should be inspired and guided by the main decisions of the Second Vatican Council. While there are different interpretations of the Council and the reform it still calls for, the

Editorial

new Pope is demonstrating, in practical and symbolic actions and in his decisions, complete openness to a reform in the spirit of the Council.

Third, reform has not been just a matter of words, or quotations from texts, but is taking shape at the most varied levels, notably as regards the necessary preparation for a wide-ranging review of the very structures of the Roman Curia. Paul VI and John Paul II, each in his own way, adapted the Curia to Vatican II and the new code of canon law but, as we show in this issue of *Concilium*, these measures were not sufficient or in accordance with the Council's ideas. Hence the need to air possibilities and present proposals for a reform of the Curia and the Church's government that are closer to the Second Vatican Council's pastoral decisions.

Because the reform of the Roman Curia is a priority at this beginning of Pope Francis's pontificate, in this issue *Concilium* offers its readers a coherent set of contributions in its tradition of publishing material rooted in the heritage of Vatican II. Pope Francis is certainly receiving countless suggestions, and anyway there are bodies in the Church with the authority and competence to provide them. In its particular sphere, the journal *Concilium* decided to invite specialists in areas such as the history of the Church, canon law, ecclesiology, pastoral ministry and spirituality to offer analyses and suggestions on the topic of reform of the Roman Curia in the light of the texts of Vatican II and later papal documents. Among the various specialists represented here, we have the pastoral sensitivity of a bishop with experience in the reality of relations between a bishops' conference and the Roman Curia, and the diplomatic arm of the Holy See in the shape of the apostolic nunciatures. We also have the ecumenical perspective provided by a Lutheran theologian known for his role as chair of the main body of the World Council of Churches.

The Roman Curia is the most ancient and longest-lasting bureaucracy in history and it has always been vigorous and active, although it has taken different forms. The second millennium of our era saw the Church's central bureaucracy begin a process of growth and centralization. The problem is that the Roman Curia seems to have remained stuck in the seventeenth century, imprisoned in a pre-Enlightenment and pre-modern model, so that the result of the reforms carried out in the twentieth century was merely to carry out the adaptation required by the separation of the Church from the Papal States, without abandoning the centralizing pressure inherent in that process. As a result, one of the questions asked today is how we can move from a sacral, pre-modern court to a functional service bureaucracy compatible with the reality of a world of citizens.

The points our authors have in common are illuminating and form an impressive common denominator: they all call for a Roman Curia at the service of the Pope and the episcopal college, since it is this college, in union with its head, the Pope, that is responsible for governing the Church. The Council as inspiration and guideline for the government of the Church has led to a vigorous revival of the ecclesiology of the episcopal college. If we are to follow this ancient ecclesiology, the Roman Curia cannot be between the Pope and the bishops and above the bishops. The bishops, scattered round the world and operating together in regional bodies at different levels, find their universal unity, as is well known, in the leadership of the Bishop of Rome, and the Roman Curia is at the service of this unity of the episcopal college headed by the Bishop of Rome. To make this repositioning effective, the Roman Curia needs to take the steps that the bishops took after Vatican II, and which Benedict XVI has now taken as Bishop of Rome. In other words, a distinction and separation between mission and person have to be made throughout the Curia. The issue with the Curia is not merely one of age limits, health or length of service, but of preventing the Curia from continuing to act as a hierarchy situated above the bishops. This is a crucial question with many implications. It leads us to ask why a lay-person possessing the appropriate required skills cannot be Secretary of State. Why is it impossible for the Congregation for Religious Institutes to be led by a wise and experienced religious sister when we know that round the world, of every four religious, three are women? Why cannot women with the proper credentials be nuncios, since there are already women ambassadors who make equally effective political representatives? At root all this amounts to a single question: Why maintain in a state of fusion, if not confusion, a priestly hierarchy and a curial bureaucracy? Isn't this what leads to a sacralization of the bureaucracy?

Modern times have been teaching us that the principle of subsidiarity can be of benefit when applied to church government. The separation of different types of powers (legislative, executive and judiciary) makes the power of each less absolute and less liable to arrogance or corruption. When we bear in mind that only God is absolute, the exercise of power in a human way, as Jesus himself taught by word and example, consists in delegation of power 'with spirit' and power 'of mission'. It is thus linked to

Editorial

the ministry and not to persons independently of their missions. Perhaps, in current, more secular terminology, power is above all empowerment or what Hannah Arendt defined so well: the capacity for action in common. This means that powerful people or power structures are those which help other people to feel that they have power. In more spiritual terms, power might be defined as the capacity for communion, or the action of the Spirit through people and structures that produces communion.

Reshaping the Roman Curia as a structure better suited to the service of the episcopal college in a communion of unity with the Pope needs to be matched by more effective instruments of government by the episcopal college. Strengthening episcopal conferences and the continental episcopal confederations should be one of the aims. The conferences, half a century after the Council, remain limited, restricted and even diminished, unable to develop all their pastoral potential. A crucial question, already analyzed by Hervé Legrand in *Concilium* 2005/4, is that of the contradictions that exist at some points between the conciliar documents, which did not lay down many rules, and the 1983 code of canon law, which remains structurally more monarchical than collegial. Furthermore, we should not forget that, according to the Second Vatican Council, it is the synod of bishops that represents the most global exercise of collegiality in the government of the Church. These questions are addressed in different ways in this issue of *Concilium*, sometimes more critically and sometimes more in the form of suggestions intended to streamline the synod process as an instrument of government in the hands of the Pope. There seems to be a consensus among the various writers that none of these governance structures has been given sufficient status since Vatican II. On the contrary, they have lost status, were diminished or diminished themselves for reasons that were as much ideological as administrative. Finally, among the other aspects of the collegial system, the college of cardinals itself is discussed here in terms of its potential as a senate of communion, and the council of eight cardinals that is currently helping the Pope with the government of the Church may go down in history as an example of good practice.

It is crucial to ask what, in the last resort, a governing college and a bureaucracy in the Church are for. The purpose of the Church is evangelization, and Pope Francis has insisted on the urgent need to exorcise the danger of a 'self-referential', self-absorbed Church. The Church's mission implies going out to the existential margins of human beings in the world, whether individual or social, all the more since

Editorial

communion with the poor is part of following Jesus. As Pope Francis has proclaimed, it is better to be a Church that has accidents because it is out and about than a Church that gets sick because it stays self-enclosed and surrenders to suffocation. The Church's government and its service structures, starting with the Roman Curia, need to set their course against this wider horizon. It is their greatest spiritual and pastoral strength.

The editors of this issue of *Concilium* are deeply grateful for the positive response they have received from the various authors, all the more so since the deadlines were particularly tight as a result of the decision to make the publication date coincide with the first working sessions of the council of cardinals set up by Pope Francis. We are pleased to have this opportunity to offer the Church this series of reflections on a topic that many Christians, and Catholics in particular, believe to be of burning and promising relevance. We put forward these contributions, historical, ecclesiological, from canon law, pastoral experience and spirituality, to aid the discussion and the 'journey together' on which Pope Francis invited us to set out on his first appearance as bishop of Rome.

Luiz Carlos Susin, Susan Ross, Silvia Scatena
Translated by Francis McDonagh

Part One: Lessons from History

Reform of the Roman Curia through History

NORMAN TANNER SJ

I Introduction

The Roman Curia has always been in need of reform, and surely always will be. *Ecclesia semper reformanda est*, so *Curia Romana semper reformanda est*. Most popes and officials of the Curia have been wise and humble enough to recognize this ongoing need. But the New Testament provides no clear model of the ideal papal Curia to which reforms might return. Peter allowed himself to be advised by Paul, who 'opposed him to his face' (Gal. 2.11), and we may assume that he accepted assistance from others (his 'Curia', perhaps including an amanuensis to write his letters), when he confronted delicate issues such as circumcision and diet.

Peter introduces us, however, to one glaring problem regarding reform of the Roman Curia. Reform normally implies return to some original, ideal arrangement: re-forming. In the case of the Curia, however, there was no clear and original arrangement to which return could be made. Christ himself said nothing explicit on the matter, at least nothing that has been recorded, and the developments under Peter were few and more personal than institutional. With the Roman Curia, therefore, we are faced squarely with the delicate issue of the relationship between Scripture and tradition.

This article is divided into five periods: the first millennium until the beginning of the East–West schism in 1054; the Middle Ages until 1300, a period of notable growth in the papal Curia; the late Middle Ages, beginning with the Avignon papacy and leading into the Renaissance papacy; the Counter-Reformation and its aftermath; and from the loss of the Papal States in 1870 until today.

II   Until 1054

The papal Curia remained small during the first millennium of Christian history. Institutional reforms are hard to pinpoint because we are dealing more with a *familia* than with a well-defined institution. The bishops of the seven suburban sees, as well as senior priests and deacons in the parishes of the city, were sometimes called 'cardinals' because they were 'hinges' (Latin *cardo* = hinge) of the Roman Church and they assisted the Pope with advice and other help. In addition, there was the more immediate papal household. At least from the time of Leo in the fifth century, most popes were careful to preserve important correspondence. We know of a small number of officials related to the drawing up and preservation of this correspondence: *amanuenses* or secretaries, as well as those responsible for the authentication and sealing of the letters, and archivists. Therefore we may presume that there were changes or 'reforms' in their duties from time to time, even though we have few precise details. We can well imagine Pope Gregory (590–604), a prolific correspondent, making changes of this kind.

Another very important dimension of the Roman Curia was that of papal legates, principally those sent to ecumenical councils. Popes were present in person at none of the seven (or eight) such councils held during the first millennium: Nicaea I in 325, Constantinople I in 381, Ephesus in 431, Chalcedon in 451, Constantinople II in 553, Constantinople III in 680–1, Nicaea II in 787, and the disputed Constantinople IV in 869–70; but they were represented at almost all of them by their legates: usually priests (though bishops were among them), and numbering two or three. Their rôles were very important: normally, though not always, they presided at the council meetings and were expected to approve the conciliar decrees.

These papal legates almost always acted correctly, but not at the Council of Ephesus in 449, where they represented Pope Leo I. At this meeting they approved, in the Pope's name, the Monophysite teaching of the Council as well as its deposition of the Patriarch of Constantinople, Flavian. The legates' ignorance of Greek, the language of the Council, may partly explain their error. On their return to Rome, however, they were roundly rebuked by Pope Leo, who disowned the Council and its ecumenical status, famously calling it a 'robber Council' (*Latrocinium*). Here we witness perhaps the most radical 'reform' of the Roman Curia in its history: not just reorganization or improvement, but rather the Pope's radical rejection of decisions made by its senior officials.

Papal legates presided, too, at some local councils, and represented the Pope on other high-level occasions, such as royal weddings or other dealings with monarchs. They were 'one-off' appointments, yet their regularity implies a certain institutional continuity. Papal representation, however, was permanent in Constantinople towards the end of the millennium, through legates who could treat with both Emperor and Patriarch. Continuous or organic development, rather than reform, describes this evolution and there were no dramatic 'about-turns', as after the Latrocinium of Ephesus. The most dramatic confrontation came when the papal legate Cardinal Humbert excommunicated Patriarch Cerularius of Constantinople in 1054, leading to a lasting schism between Rome and Constantinople. But in this case there was no dramatic 'reform' of the Roman Curia. Instead the papacy supported the action of its legate.

III Middle Ages to 1300

Soon after the beginning of the schism in 1054 there occurred the reform movement that is associated especially with Pope Gregory VII (1073–85), the 'Gregorian Reform'. Though the movement had repercussions on the Catholic Church's relations with the Orthodox and other separate Churches, it concerned reform primarily within the Catholic Church: reform of the relationship between the papacy and secular rulers in Western Christendom. The papacy sought a return to what it considered an earlier and more apostolic relationship, reversing subsequent trespasses of kings and other temporal rulers on the rights of the Church. The Roman Curia was soon brought into the equation. If the papacy were to enforce this stronger and more interventionist policy, it would need assistance from an active and well-organized Roman Curia. The results, for the Curia, were a mixture of expansion and reform.

The changes were under way even before the accession of Gregory VII and continued afterwards. Departments (*dicasteri*, as they came to be called) and their functions within the Curia came to be distinguished more clearly: the *Cancelleria* for writing and sealing papal correspondence; the *Camera* for the private arrangements of the Pope; and the *Penitenceria* for indulgences and the sacrament of penance. An important addition in the thirteenth century was the Inquisition for dealing with heresy, though its links with the Curia remained indirect until the sixteenth century. It functioned through papal commissions to individuals, mainly Dominican and Franciscan friars, to deal with heresy in a particular area, rather than as a centralized institution within the Roman Curia.

Alongside these institutional reforms, there were also calls for moral reform. As the Roman Curia grew in size and importance, calls of this second kind became more apparent and vocal. Most famously, the vigorous and saintly Bishop of Lincoln, Robert Grosseteste, travelled in 1250 from England to Lyons in France, where Pope Innocent IV and his Curia were staying, in order to protest against their venality and abuse of power. Instead of concentrating on the saving of souls, he lamented, they focused on the arts of secular administration; consequently, the papacy, which should be the sun of the whole world, was in danger of becoming the Antichrist. The Pope listened to the bishop but seemed unconvinced that the proposed reforms were necessary.

IV Late Middle Ages

Concerns about the Roman Curia, and calls for its reform, accompanied the vicissitudes of the papacy in the fourteenth and fifteenth centuries.

For almost seventy years, between 1309 and 1370, the papacy was based in Avignon in Southern France. The huge palace, which can still be seen today in remarkable preservation, was built in the city to house the Pope and his Curia. Nothing as extensive for the papal Curia had existed in Rome. Muslim advances within the Mediterranean world had reduced Rome to the edge of western Christendom, whereas Avignon was much more central. In terms of climate and orderliness, too, Avignon seemed preferable. The papal palace there may have symbolized the intended permanence of the papacy in this new location, but it also raised questions about the nature of the papacy and the papal Curia. It indicated that the Pope was principally sovereign of all Christians rather than Bishop of Rome, and it was the papal Curia rather than a Roman Curia that assisted him.

The Curia in Avignon was noted for its size and efficiency. In size, indeed, it was proportionally, in terms of the Catholic population, much larger than the Roman Curia today, which is sometimes criticized as too large. That is to say, for a total Catholic population (excluding therefore members of the Orthodox and other separate Churches) which may be estimated at some 60 million in 1300, the papal Curia in Avignon numbered

Reform of the Roman Curia through History

some 500 members, therefore one for every 120,000 Christians; whereas the Roman Curia today numbers approaching 3000 members for over one billion Catholics (1.167 billion in 2010, according to official Vatican statistics; see *The Tablet*, 27 February 2010, p. 31), therefore one member for around 400,000 Catholics.

The efficiency of the Curia in Avignon was admired, but some commentators felt it was becoming almost an end in itself. Many thought there was too much nepotism and clientilism among its members, too much attention to the paying of fees for services performed or favours granted, too much luxury and decadent lifestyle, and that it was too dominated by the French nation, to which all seven popes of the period belonged as well as most of the cardinals and other curial officials. But we should be cautious in accepting these criticisms. Many of them came later, from those who wished to discredit the Avignon papacy and avoid any return there after the papacy had settled again in Rome. When in Rome, moreover, most of the popes and curial officials had been Italians. Therefore the Avignon papacy was following the same trend, *mutatis mutandis*. Also, much of the criticism came from England, which was fighting the Hundred Years War with France and therefore lacking in appreciation of French virtues.

The Avignon papacy was followed by the long papal schism from 1370 to 1417, when two and later three popes, each with his respective Curia, vied for authority. Criticism for failing to end the schism, however, was directed largely against the claimants to the papacy rather than towards their Curias. Indeed cardinals and other members of the Curias played a major rôle in resolving the schism by facilitating its termination at the Council of Constance and the successful election of Pope Martin V.

Calls for reform of the Curia re-surfaced during the period before the beginning of the Protestant Reformation in 1517. Nevertheless, during this time, too, criticism was directed more against the popes (principally for their immoral and worldly life-styles) than the Roman Curia. Here too, however, we should beware of attributing more to the epoch than to hindsight. That is to say, much of the criticism of the Renaissance papacy and the Roman Curia came after 1517: from Protestant reformers, obviously; and, more subtly, from Catholics of the Counter-Reformation, who saw the decadence of the late medieval papacy as a means of explaining (without justifying) the awkward fact of Protestant success.

Norman Tanner SJ
V Counter-Reformation and afterwards

Should this section be headed 'Counter-Reformation', the traditional heading for this period in the history of the Catholic Church, or the more recently advocated 'Catholic Reformation' or 'early modern Catholicism'? Inasmuch as the Roman Curia was reorganized in good measure precisely to ensure that it might respond more effectively to the Protestant Reformation, 'Counter-Reformation' is surely the more appropriate heading. But how appropriate is the word 'reform'? The resulting reorganization may be termed 'reform' in the sense that it re-formed the institution, or formed it anew, but not in the sense that it returned the Curia to earlier arrangements. Instead, the new challenges of the sixteenth century spurred the changes. What was the balance between the institutional and the personal? The motivation was principally for institutional change (restructuring the departments of the Curia), but personal reform was also sought: that is, more edifying and austere life-styles, away from the somewhat luxurious living of earlier Renaissance times.

The first major reform concerned the Inquisition. In 1542, when the Protestant Reformation already held the allegiance of almost half of Europe, Pope Paul III reorganized and centralized the medieval institution, giving it the name *Sacra Congregatio Romanae et Universalis Inquisitionis seu Sancti Officii* (sometimes abbreviated in English to 'Holy Office'). Its headquarters, since the late sixteenth century, has been the fine building in Rome in the Piazza del S. Ufficio, to the left of St Peter's Church. There have been changes of name, to *Sacra Congregatio Sancti Officii* in 1908, to *Sacra Congregatio pro Doctrina Fidei* in 1965, and more recently to the simpler *Congregatio pro Doctrina Fidei* or (in the now customary Italian) *Congregazione per la Dottrina della Fede*. There have also been changes of procedure, such as the abolition of torture, but there has been remarkable institutional continuity alongside these reforms.

Other new congregations of the Roman Curia emerged in the wake of the Council of Trent. The *Congregatio Concilii* was notable. It was established in 1564, the year after the Council's conclusion, with the task of ruling on disputed points of interpretation regarding the conciliar decrees. *Congregatio Indicis Librorum Prohibitorum* was established in 1571 with the task of task of drawing up a list, or Index, of books that Catholics were forbidden to read. This work effectively came to an end only in 1965, when the list and penalties were 'suspended' (though not formally abolished).

An enduring reorganization of the Curia was inaugurated by Pope Sixtus

V in 1588. Indeed this Pope is considered to have been the founder of the modern Roman Curia. The reform established 15 congregations. Six were responsible for the government of the Papal States (the large territory in the middle of Italy belonging to the papacy), and nine had responsibility for various other dimensions of the Church. Each congregation was normally headed by a cardinal, as before, but Pope Sixtus's reform had the effect of tying the cardinals resident in Rome even more closely into the papacy, thus preventing any recurrence of their semi-independence of the type that had occurred during the papal schism and the conciliar movement in the late Middle Ages. The Holy Office was given precedence among the 15 congregations, a position which it held until 1908, when it gave way to the Secretariat of State.

The establishment of the *Congregatio de Propaganda Fide* by Pope Gregory XV in 1622 was very important. 'Propaganda' had worldwide authority: in Europe, over those countries which had left the Catholic fold and embraced the Reformation, such as the Netherlands, Britain, Scandinavia and much of Germany; and in most countries outside Europe, which were considered mission territories. Within these lands the authority of Propaganda was very extensive (it included the appointment of bishops), and long-lasting in that it endured until a certain stability for the Catholic Church had been achieved in the country. The new Congregation was thus both timely and realistic: it faced up to the enduring reality of the Protestant Reformation as well as the global expansion of Christianity following the European 'discovery' of the New World. It also came to be very well endowed financially, thus enabling the Congregation to promote a wide range of apostolic works, including seminaries. Perhaps the down side was that bishops in its territories felt too dependent on the instructions of Propaganda, and such ties of dependence partly explain why bishops from mission lands were surprisingly quiet in the early stages of Vatican II.

These were progressive developments, but they were also conservative reforms in the sense of recapturing the original inspiration of the papal Curia. Christ had told his disciples: 'Go therefore and make disciples of all nations' (Matt. 28.19); Peter had left his native country to come to Rome; and the authority of the Bishop of Rome, facilitated by the papal Curia, had gradually spread around the Mediterranean world and into Northern Europe. Accordingly, the massive geographical expansion of the Catholic Church, from the sixteenth century onwards, was accompanied by a revival or restoration of this early missionary nature of the Roman Curia.

Rome was occupied by Napoleon's army in 1796, and Pope Pius VI was taken away, to die in Valence in France in 1796. His successor Pius VII was elected in Venice and was able to return to Rome only in 1814. This turbulent period greatly impacted the Roman Curia, which was able to function only with much difficulty. Subsequently, however, the Curia grew in size while returning to earlier arrangements. Thus its development somewhat paralleled that of the Catholic monarchies which were restored after the Treaty of Vienna in 1815. Most notably, *Congregatio de Propaganda Fide* grew steadily in competence with the spread of the Catholic Church in mission lands. Its work was encouraged especially by Pope Gregory XVI (1831–46), who had been Prefect of the congregation before his election as Pope. Other territories passed from the competence of Propaganda to that of other congregations in the Curia, as episcopal hierarchies and other aspects of the Church were formally established in them: in England, for example, with the restoration of the hierarchy in 1850.

VI 1870 until today

The final loss of the Papal States in 1870, including the city of Rome, to the forces of Italian unification, had obvious implications for the Roman Curia. The results may be seen as both development and reform. There was development in the obvious sense that the papacy, and therefore the Roman Curia, had to confront a radically-changed situation. But there was reform, too, in the sense that the papacy's loss of temporal sovereignty re-formed the Curia more in the image of what it had been earlier, before the acquisition of the Papal States under Pope Gregory I (590–604).

The transition was painful for the papacy and the Roman Curia, especially for Pope Pius IX (1846–78), and it was only with the Lateran Treaty in 1929, through the initiative of Benito Mussolini and Pope Pius XI, that the papacy finally came to terms with the new situation. The prolonged unwillingness of the papacy to accept the *fait accompli* had placed many Catholics in a very difficult situation, especially in Italy.

However, various adjustments to the Curia were made during this transition period. Pope Pius X's reorganization of the Curia in 1908 was particularly important. *Dicasteri* (congregations) concerned with the government of the Papal States, which had numbered six in Pope Sixtus

V's reform of 1588, became redundant. The total number of congregations was reduced from 20 to 11, and precedence among them was transferred from the Holy Office to the Secretariat of State.

Various factors have affected the Roman Curia since the reforms of Pius X, although the organizational framework established then has remained largely intact. In terms of population, Catholics have increased from some 200 million in the world's population of 1.2 billion in 1870 (estimate of the French bishops at the First Vatican Council, see *Collectio lacensis*, vii, 845–6) to the estimated 1.167 billion out of 7 billion in 2010. This is dramatic growth (though the proportion, in terms of the world's population, has remained remarkably constant at around 17 per cent) and it has occurred especially outside Europe.

Changes in the wider world beyond Europe have been qualitative too: political independence, growing self-sufficiency on the part of local churches, the establishment of indigenous hierarchies, and much else. All this has required adaptation on the part of the Roman Curia and a huge increase in its work-load. The demands have been felt most immediately in the Secretariat of State, which has multiplied the number of nunciatures to keep abreast of newly-independent and other countries seeking papal representation, but the other *dicasteri* have been much affected too.

In various ways the Roman Curia has become both more and less worldly since 1870. It is less worldly in the obvious sense that it no longer has to concern itself with defending the temporal kingdom of the Papal States. But it is more worldly on account of the Catholic Church's expansion into a truly worldwide institution, and because, paradoxically, the loss of the temporal kingdom has led to greater and more worldwide interest in the Church's spiritual and humanitarian message. This change was seen in the activity of the papacy and Roman Curia during the two World Wars and other conflicts of the twentieth century; through the great ecumenical Council of the twentieth century, Vatican II, and its generally favourable reception worldwide; and in the internationalization of the personnel of the Roman Curia at all levels, especially during the last half century, and most notably in its last three heads, Pope John Paul from Poland, Pope Benedict from Germany, and Pope Francis from (as he said himself) 'the other end of the world'.

VII Conclusion

The Roman Curia has a remarkably long and full history. It is the longest-running bureaucracy in world history. In a sense its mission has been simple: to be at the service of the Bishop of Rome and thus serve Catholics and (very importantly, though less directly) other Christians and the whole of humanity. Within this simplicity, however, history has provided many complexities. This short essay has, I hope, provided some reflections on how the Roman Curia has coped both with its simplicity of purpose and with the complexity of reality: on how Scripture and tradition, as well as sanctity and human frailty, have been woven together by the members of this very remarkable institution.

Bibliography

The reference material for this essay and its wider context are most easily found in N. Tanner, *New Short History of the Catholic Church*, London & New York, 2011; translations into various languages have been published or are forthcoming. There is also much relevant material in Paul Van Geest & Roberto Regoli (eds), *Suavis Laborum Memoria: Chiesa, Papato e Curia Romana tra storia e teologia: Scritti in onore di Marcel Chappin SJ per il suo 70 compleanno*, Vatican City, 2013.

Reform of the Curia at and after Vatican II

MASSIMO FAGGIOLI

I Introduction

This article focuses on the question of the Roman Curia at three important points: the Second Vatican Council (preparatory phase and celebration), the papacy of Paul VI (especially *Regimini ecclesiae universae*, 1967) and the papacy of John Paul II (especially *Pastor bonus*, 1988). The post-conciliar reforms of the Curia picked up only partially on the Council's ecclesiological innovations; they worked on a structure that was still the one set up by Pope Sixtus V in 1588. The Montinian reform in particular seems to be a legacy of Pius XII's papacy, rather than of Vatican II. In a certain sense, the question of the Roman Curia has to start again from where it was at Vatican II.

II The question of the Roman Curia at Vatican II

The 1908 reform was aware that the end of the Papal States had consequences for the government of the Church. Nevertheless, the centralization of papal government on Rome reached its zenith under Pope Sarto (Pius X).[1] By the mid-twentieth century, the chief problem was still the gap between the increasing globalization of the Catholic Church and the unchanging nature of the apparatus of the congregations in the face of this epochal change. Accordingly, the curial institutions (especially the congregations and tribunals) became litigants at Vatican II, both legally and theologically: the case concerned not only the relationship between the bishops and the government of dioceses, but, especially, the relationship between the bishops and the primacy, and the function of the Curia within that relationship.

In the pre-preparatory and preparatory phases of the Council (1959–62), considerable space was given to the need to 'internationalize' the Roman Curia, and to the question of excessive centralization of the government of the universal Church. In the *vota* [responses, suggestions] sent by bishops to Rome in 1959–60, a significant number of conciliar Fathers (92) had also raised the question of papal legates. But, given the number of *vota* on the subject, much more space had to be given to the problem of the relationship with the Roman Curia and the definition of the rights of bishops in relation to those of the curial congregations and of nuncios and apostolic delegates. The *vota* sent to Rome demanded a definition and reinforcement of the powers of bishops, as against those of the Roman Curia and nuncios, so that bishops would no longer be considered '*meros mandatarios ... cum detrimento iurisdictionis eorum ordinariae ex iure divino provenientis*' [mere agents to the detriment of their ordinary jurisdiction deriving from divine law].[2] There was an avalanche of *vota* in favour of the powers of diocesan bishops: for the lightening of their bureaucratic workload; for the 'stabilization' of the five-year powers granted by the consistorial congregation of the Curia; for a broadening of powers of dispensation from the general laws of the Church; for administrative decentralization to limit appeals to the Holy See; and for the granting of greater powers to bishops in penitential discipline and in matrimonial cases, in the administration of church property and in liturgical matters.[3]

With the arrival in Rome of bishops from every continent, the beginning of the Council in October 1962 strengthened the demand for a re-alignment between centre and periphery in the Church. At a Council held in Rome and organized by the Roman Curia, from its beginning the bishops succeeded in flouting the controls imposed by the Curia, and were able to give the Council a different stamp from that hoped for by those who wanted to maintain the *status quo*. From the second day of Vatican II, with the adjournment of elections for members of the conciliar committees, the limits to the control the Roman Curia could exert over the bishops assembled from all over the world became clear. Although the first period of the Council did not deal directly with the question of the rôle of the Curia and the papacy, the experience of the Council provided a very important element in the debates during the period that followed.

In its first inter-session (January–August 1963), the Council discussed the question of the relations between centre and periphery in the co-ordinating committee. At the meeting on 26 January 1963, Cardinal Döpfner asked the Co-ordinating Committee to revise the schema *De Episcopis* [Of bishops] in Chapter 1 on the relations with the Roman congregations, in Chapter 2 on the retirement of bishops, and in Chapter 3 on bishops' conferences.

As well as the ecclesiological debate in October 1963, the Council's second session concentrated on *De Ecclesia* (then on *Lumen gentium*), but also on certain acts of Paul VI, in particular his speech to the Roman Curia on 21 September 1963. In his speech to the Curia the Pope asked for its collaboration in the reform of the central government of the Church, which was under discussion at the Council, and its support for the 'association' of residential bishops with the Roman curial congregations. At the same time, the Pope reassured members of the Curia that no reform would be made against them.[4] Council reactions to this speech varied. Some were enthusiastic, others sceptical. The judgment of Hubert Jedin, the historian of the Council of Trent, was prophetic. He believed that 'an internationalization of the Curia apparatus would mean falling from the frying pan into the fire, because experience shows that Romanized foreigners are more intolerant than Italians.'[5]

Paul VI's speech was only the opening of the debate during the 1963 Council session on the reform of the Roman Curia and its relations with the papacy. In October–November 1963, the debate on the collegiality of bishops and on *De Episcopis* represented the high point of the Council's analysis of the development of the Church's model of government. The Council opened the way for a reform of the relations between Pope, Roman Curia and bishops, on the basis of a new theological consensus, based on the collegiality of bishops and on the principle that bishops have all the necessary powers for the ordinary government of their dioceses. Besides these elements addressed in that autumn of 1963, other elements emerged in the debate and were addressed in later sessions of the Council: the consolidation of national bishops' conferences; and the re-definition of ecclesiastical boundaries, particularly of dioceses. However, a new question also arose, which was the idea of the creation of a 'council of bishops' or 'apostolic council' to support the Pope (*above* the Roman Curia) for the government of the universal Church.

However, Paul VI's ecclesiology quickly guided the debate (and, in particular, its post-conciliar canonical translation) in a more moderate direction. The *motu proprio* [papal edict or document] *Pastorale munus* of 30 November 1963, on the new powers granted to the bishops, took up some points mentioned by the bishops in the debate in the chamber, but substantially accepted the proposals contained in the documents preparatory to the Council, which had been strongly criticized by the bishops in the chamber. Paul VI responded in his own way to the pleas of the Council, but also to the intimidation by conservative sectors of the Council of the reforming majority, who accused promoters of collegiality of practising 'Jansenist episcopalism'.

Between 1964 and 1965, many observers spoke of the creation of the new 'central council of bishops' as something already at the planning stage. In Spring 1965 the question was raised whether to reform the college of cardinals and re-establish it as an organ of government of the universal Church, or whether to create a new '*Consilium centrale episcoporum*' [central council of bishops] above the Curia.[6] The Council did not follow through this initiative, but it was briefly taken up again in the years immediately after the Council, when some cardinals launched a proposal for a college of cardinals, to which presidents of national bishops' conferences would also belong.[7] Cardinal Döpfner rejected the proposal to reform the college of cardinals but supported the proposal to create a '*Consilium episcoporum*' with between 40 and 50 members (the bigger bishops' conferences would have one representative each, and the smaller ones would agree among themselves on a representative in common). These would have the function of representing the bishops and bishops' conferences to the Roman Pontiff, without curtailing the power of the primacy. Cardinal Döpfner advised giving the bishops' conferences the *ius praesentandi* [right to present], that is, the right to elect members of the 'council', each with a temporary mandate (five years), whereas the eastern patriarchs would be members by right. He also advanced the proposal to include in the council the prefects or secretaries of ministries in the Roman Curia, in order to create a 'fruitful collaboration' between the new 'council of bishops' and the Curia. Döpfner was also speaking in the name of the German bishops' conference, which did not see a reform of the college of cardinals as desirable.

But during these same months Paul VI was already planning the '*Synodus episcoporum*' [synod of bishops], which Pope announced to the Council at the opening of its fourth period with *Apostolica sollicitudo* (a *motu proprio* of 15 September 1965). This was clearly a preventive measure in relation to the more radically reforming proposals of the Council, of the *De episcopis* committee, and of the draft decree *Christus Dominus*.[8] Döpfner's proposals on the creation of a 'limited bishops' council' above the Roman Curia was not accepted by the Pope. The way chosen by Paul VI was to create a purely consultative 'synod of bishops'. This entailed the abandonment of the Council's request to create a 'council of bishops' around the Pope, and also the abandonment of the vague proposal to reform the college of cardinals as *'Senatus Romani Pontificis'* [senate of the Roman Pontiff].[9]

III   Papacy and Roman Curia in the final documents of Vatican II

In the conciliar battle between different reform plans for the central government of the Church, the idea of a 'central council of bishops' served to prepare the ground for the new body proposed by Paul VI and the Roman Curia. Meanwhile, the attempts to modernize the college of cardinals remained just rumours in the background during those final months of Vatican II. Between the election of Paul VI in June 1963 and the 1965 session, reform of the Curia became a demand by the Council, received by the Pope and entrusted to a small group of (curial) advisers, who remanded reform in the post-conciliar period, in particular to the new Codex of Canon Law. The debate on reform of the central government of the Church focused on the question of internationalizing the personnel of the Curia, on the new rôle of national bishops' conferences (also thanks to the role played by these in liturgical reform), and on the retirement of bishops on grounds of age. However, the Council was completely stymied in its attempt to deal with questions of the reform of the process of nominating bishops and the rôle of Vatican diplomacy in relation to the Roman Curia.[10]

The Church and the Roman Curia had changed between the end of the Papal States and the beginning of the twentieth century: from a Curia as organ of government of the Church and the Papal States to a Curia as organ of government of a Church which had become truly universal. It had become more interventionist on the international level and better equipped to ensure that the line decided upon by the Pope could be sent out from Rome.

Vatican II stood at the end of this trajectory of the 'long nineteenth century'. The conciliar bishops and theologians were now well beyond the mourning period for the loss of the Papal States, and many of them were also well into the next stage, that of reconsidering papal power and the power of the Roman Curia within a more complex and organic debate on power in the Church. The subject of papal power was approached at the Council mainly *'per via compensativa'* [in a compensatory way]. The ecclesiology of *ressourcement* [resourcing] through ancient biblical, patristic and liturgical sources enabled them to relativize the pronouncements of Vatican I on the primacy and infallibility of the Pope through 'episcopal collegiality'. This was inserted with great accuracy into chapter 3 of *Lumen gentium* (the Constitution on the Church (not without passing, outside the control of the chamber, through the Caudine Forks of the *Nota explicativa praevi*a [preliminary explanatory note] added by the Pope to the already approved text). But this solution presented two problems. First, the chapter on collegiality left untouched the theological and institutional chapter on the relations between the papacy and the Roman Curia. In its theology of the papacy, the Catholic Church at Vatican II succeeded in coming to terms with history, and accepted the idea that the papacy, as it is understood today, is a historical creation and there was no real Pope in the first centuries of the Church's history. However, this same standard was not used in confronting the Roman Curia. That was not only because, during the Council and its aftermath, the Roman Curia acted in its own defence much more ably than the papal power. It was also because the historical argument should have been used in a much more radical way towards the Curia, given the clear theological inconsistency of the entity 'Roman Curia', and the plain evidence of this body's origins in the Middle Ages and then in the early modern era in the government of the Church.[11] The conciliar decree *Christus Dominus* tried to combine a new theology of the papacy with reform of the Roman Curia, but remanded the reform of the Curia to the Pope himself. 'On the centre-periphery issue the minority never really lost control. It was in that regard so successful that with the aid of Paul VI, the centre not only held firm and steady but, as the decades subsequent to the Council have irrefutably demonstrated, emerged even stronger.'[12]

IV Reform of the Roman Curia in the aftermath of the Council

Pope Montini confronted the question of reform of the Roman Curia with a series of legislative acts, which tinkered with the Roman Curia created in the aftermath of the Council of Trent, but without any radical modification of the structure given to it by Sixtus V in 1588.[13]

The Holy Office changed its name with *Integrae servandae* (the *motu proprio* of 7 December 1965). With *Pro comperto sane* (the *motu proprio* of 6 August 1967), Paul VI gave residential bishops the opportunity of becoming members of ministries. But it was with the apostolic constitution *Regimini ecclesiae universae* (15 August 1967) that Paul VI set his seal on his reform of the Curia. The Curia was defined in its relation to the 'universal Church'. Four types of office were created (congregations, tribunals, councils and offices). The Secretariat of State was given a central position within the Curia. Members of the Curia were to stand down every five years (unless re-nominated) and all curial offices were automatically to lapse (expect that of the representative for the Secretariat of State) with *vacatio sedis* [vacating of the seat]. The reform came into effect on 1 January 1968. A process of internationalizing the curial personnel began (clearly visible in the nominations to the Curia of Cardinals König, Roy, Seper, Villot and Garrone between 1967 and 1969). This was followed by the general regulation of the Roman Curia (22 February 1968): retirement at age 70 for minor offices and at 75 for major offices.[14] This reform was inspired by criteria of government of the legal–rational and bureaucratic type: rationalization, centralization and uniformization.[15] But the 1967 reform reinforced the power of the Pope,[16] and in its way fulfilled 'Pius XII's dream of a centralizing reform of the Curia'.[17]

Other later acts by Paul VI confirmed the Pope's intention to pursue a middle way in reforming the central government of the Church, but always with the intention of reinforcing the liberty of the Pope, the 'reforming prince', in relation to the Curia. *Sollicitudo omnium ecclesiarum* (*motu proprio* of 24 June 1969) concerned the rôle of nuncios, and *Ingravescentem aetatem* (*motu proprio* of 21 November 1970) the retirement of cardinals from all curial offices at the age of 80. Against other suggestions formulated in the aftermath of the Council, the apostolic constitution *Romano Pontifici eligendo* (1 October 1975) confirmed the conclave as the electoral college of the Pope, and introduced an incomplete 'spoils systems' into the relationship between the papacy and the Roman Curia.

John Paul II's centralizing reform of the Curia continued to pursue the course opened up by Paul VI; it merely added some ecclesiological consistency to the changes made by Pope Montini. Firstly, the new 1983 Code of Canon Law failed to value local churches or the idea of the Church as a communion of churches. The apostolic constitution *Pastor bonus* (28 June 1988) gave the final result of the working party for the reform of the Curia set up by Paul VI in 1974. Following his election, John Paul II nominated his own committee (led by Cardinal Sabattani, prefect of the Segnatura), whose 1985 final report (just before the extraordinary synod) was not accepted. Another committee followed, the 'Baggio committee' (the members were Cardinals Arinze, Castillo Lara, Gagnon, Rossi and Stickler, under the leadership of Cardinal Baggio, the Camerlengo [Chamberlain] with another report, which gave rise to the constitution *Pastor bonus*.[18]

The inspiring principles of *Pastor bonus* were the idea of the Church as *communio* [a communion], the pastoral nature of the authority of bishops, the collegiality of Pope and bishops, the vicarious nature of the Roman Curia.[19] The reform simplified the structure of ministries and reduced their number (nine congregations, 12 councils, three offices), creating a structure of 'equals', but keeping the pre-eminence of the Secretariat of State. Greater powers were given to the Congregation for the Doctrine of Faith and, in *Pastor bonus*, as well as greater importance being given to five-yearly visits *ad limina* [bishops to visit the Pope], there was barely any mention of national bishops' conferences. The systemization and clarification of the powers of congregations was a step backwards from the 1967 reform.[20] As Cardinal Baggio said, *Pastor bonus* represented 'a revision rather than a reform'.[21]

The constitution *Pastor bonus* must be read in the context of other relevant documents to understand the ecclesiology of the long pontificate of Wojtyla–Ratzinger (1978–2013). There was also the substantial lack of government of the Curia by John Paul II, and then by Benedict XVI. During the pontificate of Benedict XVI, the only significant acts with respect to the structure and functioning of the Roman Curia were a few *motu proprios* by which Pope Ratzinger made certain modifications to the text of *Pastor bonus*, transferring some powers relative to the dispensation of ratified non-consummated marriage and cases of nullity, powers over seminaries and over catechesis. The creation of a new ministry, the Pontifical Council for the Promotion of New Evangelizations (21 September 2010), was a response to the need for theological programming, rather than to the need to rethink the Curia and its functions.

The pontificate of Benedict XVI has passed into history as the time of most serious crisis in the history of the contemporary Church, because of the authority and reputation of the Roman Curia. This fact must be examined

Reform of the Curia at and after Vatican II
in the context of 500 years of 'revisions', that is, of failed reforms.
Translated by Dinah Livingstone

Notes

1. F. Jankowiak, *La Curie Romaine de Pie IX à Pie X*, Rome, 2007, pp. 539 & 570.
2. *Acta et Documenta Concilio Oecumenico Vaticano Secundo Apparando* (AD) I/2, App. 1, pp. 422–63 (*De rationibus inter S. Sedem et Episcopos determinandis*), p. 422.
3. *Cf.* AD I/2, App. 1, pp. 428–63 (*De maiore potestate Episcopis concedenda*).
4. The Pope's speech in *Insegnamenti di Paolo VI*, vol. I (1963), Vatican City, 1964, pp. 142–51.
5. Quoted by A. Melloni in *Storia del concilio Vaticano II*, G. Alberigo (ed.), vol. 3, Bologna, 1998, p. 33.
6. *Cf.* Massimo Faggioli, *Il vescovo e il concilio. Modello episcopale e aggiornamento al Vaticano II*, Bologna, 2005, pp. 389–438.
7. *Cf.* A. Melloni, *Il conclave. Storia di un'istituzione*, Bologna, 2001, pp. 128–9.
8. *Cf. Erzbischöfliches Archiv München – Julius Kardinal Döpfner. Archivinventar der Dokumente zum Zweiten Vatikanischen Konzil*, G. Treffler & P. Pfister (eds), Regensburg, 2004, pp. 102–3.
9. *Cf.* Antonino Indelicato, *Il sinodo dei vescovi: la collegialità sospesa (1965–1985)*, Bologna, 2008.
10. *Cf.* Massimo Faggioli, *Il vescovo e il concilio, op. cit.*, passim.
11. *Cf.* Joseph Lécuyer, 'The Place of the Roman Curia in Theology', in *The Roman Curia and the Communion of Churches*, Peter Huizing & Knut Walf (eds), *Concilium* 127 (1979/7), pp. 3–11.
12. John W. O'Malley, *What Happened at Vatican II*, Cambridge, MA thesis, 2008, p. 311.
13. *Cf.* Jörg Ernesti, *Paul VI. Der Vergessene Papst*, Freiburg im Breisgau, 2012, pp. 148–51; Andrea Riccardi, *Il potere del papa da Pio XII a Giovanni Paolo II*, Rome–Bari, 1993.
14. *Cf.* A. Melloni, *Il conclave, op. cit.*, p. 132.
15. *Cf.* Hervé-Marie Legrand, 'Du gouvernement de l'Eglise depuis Vatican II', in *Lumière et Vie* 288 (Oct.–Dec. 2010), pp. 47–56.
16. *Cf.* Andrea Riccardi, 'Da Giovanni XXIII a Paolo VI', in *Chiesa e Papato nel mondo contemporaneo*, Giuseppe Alberigo & Andrea Riccardi (eds), Rome–Bari, 1990, pp. 169–285.
17. René Laurentin, 'Paul VI et l'après-concile', in *Paul VI et la modernité dans l'Église*, Rome, 1984, p. 575.
18. *Cf.* Joël-Benoît d'Onorio, *Le Pape et le gouvernement de l'église*, Paris, 1992, pp. 287–309; id., *La Curia romana: aspetti ecclesiologici, pastorali, istituzionali. Per una lettura della Pastor bonus*, Vatican City, 1989.
19. *Cf.* J. Beyer, 'Le line fondamentali della Cost. Ap. Pastor Bonus', in *La Curia Romana nella Cost. Ap. Pastor Bonus*, Piero Antonio Bonnet & Carlo Gullo (eds), Vatican City, 1990, pp. 17–43.
20. *Cf.* James Provost, 'Pastor Bonus: Reflections on the Reorganization of the Roman Curia', *The Jurist* 48 (1988), pp. 499–535.
21. Joël-Benoît d'Onorio, *Le Pape et le gouvernement de l'église, op. cit.*, p. 304.

Part Two: The Canonical and Institutional Level

Senatus Communionis: A Senate of Communion

ALBERTO MELLONI

I Introduction

The problems of the reform of the Curia and of reforming the Church were lumped together in the conclave. That focused the question on better 'management' of a structure inspired by a universalist ecclesiology. However, the crucial point of conciliar doctrine on collegiality is not the participation of more people in a universal power, but the building of a communion of local churches. Therefore a senate of communion, whether or not it is prefigured by the council of eight or less, will be decisive for this papacy. The new papacy has aroused an enthusiasm which institutional questions must now live up to.

The election of Pope Francis raised new confidence in the Church: enthusiastic, simple, sincere and universal. The conclave not only ended the widowhood of the Church of Rome that began with the brave and unusual gesture of Benedict XVI's resignation, but also opened a new season which resembles, at least *ex parte papae* [on the Pope's part] a new spring, apparently waiting at the doors of time.

II Ambivalent precedents

This is not the first time that this has happened. Even at the risk of appearing deaf to the collective sense of relief which permeated Catholicism in 2013, we may recall that similar hopes were raised by other conclaves. The conclave that elected Leo X at the beginning of the sixteenth century felt like a light in the darkness of the disfigurement of the Church.[1] The conclave from which Pius IX emerged in 1848 was thought for a time to herald a turning-point, which came to nothing and caused bitter disappointment.[2] In 1963, Giovanni Battista Montini was elected, a man who was unpopular with the 'Roman party' entrenched in the Roman Curia; for the three preceding decades he had been the target of dark manoeuvres to get rid of him. His election seemed to promise a future for Vatican II. Nevertheless it turned out to be more conflictual than was expected after that *habemus papam* ['we have a Pope'].[3]

Anyone seeking an optimistic precedent often cites the analogy between Francis and John XXIII, and in some ways that is not wrong. The accession of Roncalli, which marked the end of that period of theological 'Terror' culminating in *Humani generis* ['Of the Human Race', a papal encyclical of 1950], had a different half century behind it. That was marked by a drama of repression during which, however, theological research had been driven with even more energy by a collective sense of history and its urgencies. Such horrors and energies have been lacking for decades in current Catholic theology and for good reason.

In spite of its short length and breadth, the fact is that the papacy of Francis appears to be, or is, the first sign of spring since Vatican II. It is a 'grace upon grace' which was denied, for example at the fourth Lateran Council, overwhelmed by the political crisis of the Empire; or at the Council of Basle, where reforming hopes petered out in disputes; or at Trent, whose reforming impulse froze with the death of Borromeo. The grace in question awaits not only a sequence of individual enthusiastic responses, but a joint response, institutional in its way. The renewed papal style of Bergogolio raises a consensus which also harbours a nostalgia for a 'papolatry' silenced during the long agony of Wojtyla (John Paul II), and then by the convulsions of the reign of Ratzinger (Benedict XVI). The new Pope has raised deeper hope and more insistent demands: 'the Pope cares'. So is his way of living and expressing himself more like a parish priest sensitive to the condition of his flock, rather than like a universal bishop, only an extension of the Tridentine *suprema lex* [supreme law] for the Roman papacy? Or could his doctrinal and pastoral exegesis of Vatican II and Pope John's 'pastorality' actually extend to the ecclesial level, rather than remaining on the level of private virtue (to use the language of canonizations)?

What everyone has seen in the first months of Francis' ministry is something that relates to Pope John's intuition, but also to the trivializations to which it was subjected in the succeeding decades. His attempt to enhance authority by expressing Christian life as living simply reminds us, for example, of things that occurred at the Council, like the Pact of the Catacombs, when the bishops celebrating the end of Vatican II recommitted themselves to a way of life in accordance with the Gospel. That related to the princely daily life that was then commonplace for all prelates. It also meant the huge effort by the Fathers of the 1968 Medellín assembly to provide the Council with a growing hermeneutic: Medellín saw love of the poor in the light of the liberation brought by Jesus and his Gospel. However, these efforts fell victim to the trivializations and contradictions which brought the Roman Catholic Church to where it stood in February 2013.

III Repercussions and alibis

The papacy lost spiritual prestige in the Wojtyla and Ratzinger years, during which Rome exercised a 'policy of doctrinal power'.[4] Restoring this prestige must involve not only the peripheries but the church institutions in the quest to give doctrine a pastoral character. This cannot be a miracle depending on a single person or be delegated to one individual, even if that individual is invested with a ministry and particular grace, such as those of the Bishop of Rome. The salutary rareness of Pope Francis' behaviour impels us to ask how much theological awareness the Pope brings to actions and words which have dismissed, without even a breath of polemic, the cornerstone of the two preceding papacies: the idea that the Church gains strength by using all its strength in the public arena. But the election of Bergoglio removes any alibi even for the 'moaning' sectors of the Church, whose protests against the Council or against the papacy, against clericalism or the episcopate, appear more dated than ever today. For Bergoglio's style imposes on each and all a responsibility to live a Christian life that is much higher than the right to protest, whether these protests come, so to speak, from the right or the left of the Church.

The 'Franciscan' style of exercising the Petrine ministry repudiates the theological and institutional immobility which in the end reduced Vatican II to a basis for negotiating with the small world of Lefebvre, or to a source for citations outside the theological discourse of the Church of Rome. But it also puts in serious doubt the lazy policy of manifestos and appeals against centralism. Not because there is no centralism to deconstruct. A theologian with a life history in the Curia like Walter Kasper[5] denounced it in clear terms. But it can become just that, a policy, an ideologically opposed one, but still just a policy. A policy that would reduce the collegiality of bishops to democratization, with consequences that would be no less grave than those which, in the name of less archaic consultation procedures or planetary delocalization of the chair of Peter,[6] manage to increase centralism. That is to say, what makes the difference is not the type of procedure that derives from a univocally universalist ecclesiology. What matters is the institutions that can follow from an ecclesiology which puts the local church first: the local church as this particular community encountering Christ, and the episcopate as an expression of that ecclesial faith, and their relationship with the *norma normans* [standardizing standard] of eucharistic celebration.

Therefore the institutional content of this aged Pope's ministry is decisive (in fact it was this question of age that led the conclave to their compromise election of Francis). For obvious reasons a Pope who is nearly 80 will certainly not be able to deal with the long-term consequences of his choices. Even in view of that Council which Cardinal Martini called for in 1999[7] and which remains 'the' act of supreme government with which the Pope of Rome and the heads of the Christian Churches confront the twenty-first century, Francis will decide fairly soon on a trajectory which will have scant chances of correction *in itinere* [on the way], and which will be decided by the question: what ecclesiology determines the institutional choices he has made and will make?

IV Reforming the irreformable

This is where we find the paradox that emerged during the conclave and is one of the critical points of the next period of the pontificate of Pope Francis. In the days awaiting the *extra omnes* ['Everybody out!' – at the beginning of the conclave to elect a new Pope, everybody except the cardinals with the right to vote is ordered to leave the Sistine Chapel and the doors are shut] and those following, many cardinals said and thought that the main problem for the Church and the main mess to be sorted out was the 'reform' of the Roman Curia: a cesspit of vices which have become part of world literature, and which after centuries of stability became, from 1908 onwards, the target of continual ephemeral 'reforms'. In fact it appears to have been the incubator of those scandals and obscenities that drove Ratzinger to make his 'great refusal'. Its last two chiefs, Cardinal Angelo Sodano and Cardinal Tarciso Bertone, were the subjects of the most violent controversy. Through a clever game of insinuations and revelations, the idea arose in the Catholic world and public opinion that crude administrative solutions (a new management, a new business plan, innovations in procedure and product or perhaps getting rid of 'bad company') would be enough to heal a poisonous climate.[8] As if acting from 'outside' with inquisitorial rigour or police action, under the aegis of the New York zero-tolerance formula, could guarantee a renewal of Catholic vitality (and while they were at it, wipe out the shame caused by the fact that some of the rapists of children, referred to by the horrible euphemism 'paedophiles' [child lovers], were priests).[9]

Amid all this journalistic and ecclesiastical babble, what was lacking (although this is not surprising) was reflection on the ambiguity of the term 'reform'. For in the strict sense only what belongs to the *forma ecclesiae* [form of the Church] is subject to that *reformatio* [reformation] which is essential to Christian life once the form meant to contain it has lost its proper shape.[10] Other things are really corrections (*emendationes*) which cannot be called reforms without the awareness that they can only be effective when r*eforma ecclesiae* [reform of the Church] is their guiding light; they must be lit by the light shining from a lampstand (rather than hidden under a bushel).

V Levels of *emendatio curiae*

Accordingly, after the conclave the countdown began for the reform of the Curia, paced by the slowness with which Pope Francis makes known his choices (the Secretary of State Pietro Paroline was named at the end of August). The pace is also determined by the way in which the Pope allows lines of government to mature (in preaching he has spoken about synodality, with a clarity that has not been heard for some time, but without taking any new steps). Beyond the conjectures, this action must be articulated on three levels: that of the organogram which decides about personnel, the organizational level, which faces a plurality of options to be dealt with, and, lastly, the abovementioned ecclesiological level.

The organogram is basically simple. The Pope must dismiss anyone who needs to be dismissed, we would hope without sending him to ruin a diocese after having ruined himself. Then he must choose people (perhaps not only clergy and not only men) who, according to the old adage, seem capable of serving the Church rather than making the Church serve them. The most important step has been the recalling from Venezuela (where someone in Rome hoped he had been forgotten for at least 25 years, as happened to Amleto Giovanni Cicognani under Pius XII) of a Secretary of State oriented towards the politics of Asia. The Pope has taken and will take other decisions. These are obviously not immune from influences and mistakes, which he may not always have the time or the will to rectify.

The organizational level is harder, because it involves the complex architecture of decision-making. In terms of transparency, timeliness and global significance, the same objective can in fact be reached by combining different actions and combining procedures, times, teams and so on in different ways. What he decides about the final outcome of the *emendatio curiae* [correction of the Curia] will not, therefore, depend on the direction of this or that single decision, but on the whole system and the homogeneity that will be obtained by intervening in this or that sphere.

Merely by way of example, I shall indicate some areas of action. For instance, it is obvious that there are job descriptions in the Curia 'tailored' to a particular person, which need to be rethought with a view to reducing narcissism. Obsolete political divisions remain, like that of the Deputies, who are still just two, the same as when the world was small and there was no European Union. They also lack structures for interacting with the continental desks and the heads of congregations. There are questions of government. There are dangerous practices, like the office of cardinal being given as of right to presidents of pontifical councils. This encourages the drive to multiply and the struggle for birettas *praeter necessitatem* [beyond what is necessary]. There is an overlap of bodies (in the charity area, for example). The presence of Vatican City as a State in various assemblies requires the establishment of urgent practices of transparency in the Catholic agenda. It also prevents anything being done about the question of how to replace a bank which has been nothing but a source of woe, even when it was well administered with a simple 'Ark of Legates', an unbreakable money box from which no one except the congregations could take back money donated with or without an explicit purpose. But each of these aspects, and many more that could be mentioned, combine with the others to form 'chains' of different significance and importance.

VI Omnivorous universalism

The crux of the reform of the Curia is not about the Curia but about the Church. It relates to the doctrinal basis of the institutional modifications that the Pope wants to make in this or that area. *Pastor bonus* ['Good Shepherd'], John Paul II's 1983 reform, was based on a classic universalist ecclesiology, which produced apparently bold reforms that are in fact ephemeral.[11]

The Gregorian scheme of a handed-down universal power adopted monarchy as its model for the whole second millennium of the Latin Church. But this scheme could easily now be adapted to a participative, even democratic, political philosophy with the same efficacy and the same risk. The risk would be of a cosmetic 'modernizing' that would bring the Church more in line with the theories of power in force today. That is what happened with great anticipatory power to the theories of the centuries up to the Restoration [of European monarchies after the fall of Napoleon in 1814] and to totalitarianisms. But just as the Church cannot announce the Gospel without describing itself, once again and for that very reason, this kind of 'modernizing' would risk proclaiming the faith on the basis of its own credibility, in an insensitive and ultimately fatal reversal.

The marriage between universalism and participation (even disguised as collegiality) would continue to use the substance of the Church as a pattern of the Trinitarian unity, a necessary container which must be continually and explicitly relativized so that the proclamation of the Gospel does not set a kind of proclamation of the Church as its own premise.

However, this danger does not lack an antidote. That is an acceptance of a strong and proper collegiality, understood not as a balance to monarchy, but as the discovery that the substance of the Petrine ministry was not exhausted in the forms in which it was exercised between the eleventh and nineteenth centuries. Or better still, as that ministry which creates unity rather than division, which occurred in a small, often distorted, way from the Council of Florence onwards. Only an ecclesiology of local churches (a eucharistic ecclesiology) will be able, not to 'democratize' or constitutionalize the monarchy (as the failed project of *Lex ecclesiae fundamentalis* [fundamental law of the Church] attempted), or to assist it with a 'crown council' [monarch's privy council] (a potentially blasphemous expression because the one king is the Lord), but to develop the *communio* [communion] of the local churches *in quibus et ex quibus* [in which and out of which], as the fine formula of Vatican II puts it, the *unam sanctam* [one holy] is realized.[12]

Without reflection and an institutional elaboration of the *communio ecclesiarum* [communion of churches] and of the *communio episcoporum* [communion of bishops], reform of the Curia will be confined to limited territory, maybe even undermined.[13] It would be historically reductive to believe that the immorality emanating from the Curia was the cause and not also the effect of deeper deformities. It is a mistake to deceive ourselves that a clean-up operation could prevent a return, within a few years, to the point where it started.

VII Vocation

We need a historical–theological understanding of what the Curia has thought it should, or claimed it could, replace in the Church, in order to heal not only the Curia but the Church. This would need far-reaching research that was not subordinate to the 'system' (in Congar's meaning of the term[14]) on the cultural level. I shall limit myself here to a few examples.

The 'system' does not arise from the existence of helpers, whom the Pope obviously needs. It arises from a mentality that makes intensive use of the prerogatives of the Roman Pontiff, including those most discussed at the ecumenical level. (These, however, could acquire a very different flavour if they were understood on the basis of an ecclesiology of communion *rata et consummata* [ratified and consummated]). This mentality was already arising with the eleventh century reform, when it was no accident that the members of the college of cardinals described themselves as successors to the college of apostles. That was an abusive expansion of their function, which resurfaced in the twentieth and twenty-first centuries, when the college of cardinals was recalled by the *codex iuris canonici* [code of canon law] to its first duty to elect the Bishop of the Church of Rome. Although those 'wearing the purple' are cardinal clerics of the Church of Rome, they also happily assumed the consultative role of an eminent 'representation' of the episcopate that has no theological, ecclesiological or juridical foundation.[15]

Vatican II's teaching that it is the college of bishops as a whole and as a guarantee of communion with Peter that succeeds to the college of the apostles, did not resolve everything. Concerned to state that the college of bishops participates in co-governing the 'universal' Church, Vatican II did not close the door on the idea that is now coming back in this phase of 'reform' of the Curia. That is that power over the universal Church (whether that of the Pope *solus* [alone], or that of the college together with Peter, whether with new spokespersons or existing ones) should have an annual or monthly intensity. This means that universal power needs a Curia to serve it as its executive.[16] Such a 'collegiality' would promote a universalism that, blamelessly or otherwise, failed to regard the catholicity and hence the unity of the Church.

Therefore, in my opinion, the two formal reforms of 1967 and 1988 and the two informal ones of 1959 and 2007[17] had no effect. For without what Eugenio Carecco called 'an ecclesiological soul', which can only be the *communio ecclesiarum* [communion of churches], any reform becomes merely a revision of the organogram, job shuffling, engineering maintenance that bypasses the crucial points of the problem, particularly the strictly institutional ones.

Resistance to setting up a body that represents the college as an organ of *communio episcoporum* [communion of bishops], as well as of *communio ecclesiarum* [communion of churches], is associated with the recent expansion of the duties of the college of cardinals. Or with the idea that the best person of all to 'do' collegiality is the Pope, because he universalizes what was closed off,[18] or can spend more time with the churches by journeys which air travel makes it possible to increase. Against this sort of papal Pentecostalism, we need to recover the old, healthy 'Latin' faith in institutions, because that kind of wisdom also remembers that every good intention becomes fragile when it presumes to do without the purely institutional dimension, which is the backbone within the flesh of a Church that is ever ready to become too proud.

It is obvious with this umpteenth reform or emendation of the Roman Curia that, as in all those of preceding centuries (from Urban II onwards), the matter of *money* will be painful and basic, persons are essential, and procedures have a weight.

This requires that communion should not just be a vague objective to which the action of what already exists should be related, but that it should be expressed iconically in an organ of communion, expression and guarantee of that ecclesiological soul, which is able to deal with three key points for church reform: collegiality, poverty and unity.[19] On poverty Francis has shown immediately that he does not feel the distinctions are important (between poor church, church of the poor, church for the poor). But he does not and cannot think that the Church's poverty can be reduced to a bit of restraint in the Vatican style. On unity Pope Francis has great advantages. He will be returning to Jerusalem in the footsteps of Paul VI and Athenagoras, where intercommunion seemed at its closest. He might take the Holy Shroud to Moscow as an act of penance by a Church that has doubted the qualifications of Churches of other traditions. He might be the one, half a millennium after the Reformation, to ask whether the 1999 agreement on justification between Evangelicals and Roman Catholics should be confined to theological manuals. But all this would make sense only if it was not an exploit in the Wojtylian manner, designed to grace the most uplifting chapters of his biography. It must be directed towards the growth of love between Christian people. It cannot be just the sophisticated virtuosity of a professional theology or disillusioned politeness between ancient heads of divided Churches.[20]

VIII A body of eight

With that said, it remains up to Francis to decide whether to be the last Pope to evade the collegiality of Vatican II, or a different Pope who is the first consciously to implement it in the Catholic Church. The starting-point he inherits does not need clarifying because it stands at zero. For decades the Church has been clothed in zero collegiality and this has aroused acute nostalgia. As an excellent book by Antonino Indelicato has shown, by paying attention to the Jesuit fathers Bortolotti and Tucci, the synod of bishops could become an organ of embryonic collegiality. But it has become the semblance of a collegiality that does not exist.[21] What must we think of the respect Peter has for the college if we are to believe that a body without power of action, without deliberative capacity, without any voice about its length, expresses that college which, together with and under Peter, exercises full and supreme power in the Church? Nevertheless, that synod of bishops, which is little more than an agreeable aspect of exchange, is enough to arouse the joy of communion in every bishop, even though their meeting lacks both the tone and the dignity which the venerable name of synod demands.[22]

The beginning of effective collegiality in the Roman Church may have already been put in place by Pope Francis with the body of eight which he set up in June and which met in October 2013; it gives him a *consilium* [council], not only for the reform of the Curia, but *ad gubernandum ecclesiam* [to govern the Church].[23] For months there was no sign to indicate its nature and powers. All that was known was that Cardinal Maradiaga would be its co-ordinator and an Italian Bishop Semeraro would be secretary. That reinforced the suspicion that this group was just an ordinary pontifical commission with consultative functions, or at most the 'crown council' that, in the horrible formulation, would exorcise the 'spectre' of collegiality and synodality in the name of a political philosophy of the monarchical kind. Then, on 30 September a chirograph finally appeared which declared some intentions.[24] There was to be a permanent body, variable in configuration, but with precise duties. In the June communiqué, apart from reform of the Curia, there was talk of a rôle of 'advising [the Pope] in the government of the universal Church'. However, in the chirograph it says they will be 'consulted on 'questions that from time to time' are deemed 'worthy of attention', and that this 'group of cardinals' will be an expression of two aspects: on the one hand of 'episcopal communion', and, on the other, of 'help to the *munus petrinum* [office of Peter, that is, the headship of the Roman Catholic Church: the papacy], which the episcopate scattered throughout the world can provide. Hence there are two functions: one relating to collegiality, and the other to forms of exercising the Petrine ministry.

Despite its prudence and deliberately reserved language, the chirograph shows the eight to be an initial organ of episcopal collegiality, even though this body is composed of bishops chosen by the Pope alone, expressly to escape from a five-hundred-year-old impasse. The immediate over-insistence, with which a certain influential commentator hastened to say (on who knows what basis) that 'then the Pope decides on his own' shows that this breaking out of the circle that closed off any progress towards an embryonic implementation of collegiality in the church of Rome has aroused reactionary alarm.

In fact, it is not the way in which it is set up which makes a body constitutional (as the electoral system of the synod of bishops demonstrates from the contrary). Obviously, escaping from a consensus on names, with classical rules *de maioritate* [of majority], could give the body more authority. But waiting for the construction of a complex agreement on the formation of consensus would mean relegating *sine die* the passage from government by the Pope alone to government by the Pope and the college with the Pope, for which Vatican II considered it had produced the ecclesiological basis.

IX   A senate of communion

Nevertheless, the constitution of a *senatus communionis* [senate of communion] as an expression of the communion of the churches (even supposing while not granting there was a will, as at Vatican II, to recover the word 'college' and also the word 'senate' from the vocabulary of the cardinalate), now after 50 years of inconclusive work, needs a maieutic action of a primatial kind: the Pope must act as midwife. Once he has the eight or another instrument, if the former proved inadequate to the task, the Pope will have initiated the setting up of a collegial practice in the government of the Church. The synodal functioning of a senate of communion could be based on four options. I shall try to offer a possible practical articulation, merely by way of example, because, as I said, I do not believe that it will be pressure groups or 'backseat drivers' who help to unblock a stagnant situation that has lasted for half a century.

The *first option* is for a theological or 'angelical' geography of the world, which a spiritual rather than spiritualist vision always sees as the articulation of languages and cultures. A collegial body must give voice to the churches in their own particularity or rather, to use the language of Revelation, to their 'angels'. This could 'represent'[25] a geography (which might also be reflected in the reform of the deputies of the Secretariat of State?) which does not follow the Olympic logic of 'continents', but the real spiritual and historical profiles of Christian life (for example, keeping North America distinct from Central and South America).

The *second option* concerns ways of working. Because the senate of communion is a body and not one of the thousand useless Roman assemblies, it must have a regular meeting schedule and give its members, not the right but the duty, to create its agenda. This could cover more delicate questions like the way of electing bishops, the choice between defending the ministry and defending celibacy, the restoration of penance after the abandonment of auricular confession, the role of nuncios and so on. This work could also include setting up consultative groups, guidance procedures, delegation of work, and synods of bishops, who would draw up not only the subjects but the style of approach that needs to be practised in order to be valued.

The *third option* relates to the quantity and quality of the presence of the Pope. The senate of communion must not be a place where the Pope goes if he has the time, but the body of which he is a member and also the head, with all the prerogatives and duties this entails. In fact, it will be the Pope who decides whether to submit a question to the senate, the college or no one. He will be the one to decide how to bring forward the most important matters in effective dialogue with his brothers. But, as convenor, he must also give of himself and open up a practice which reduces adulation and increases truth.

The *fourth option* concerns the quality and quantity of autonomy of the senate in relation to the Roman Curia. In my opinion, a body of communion ought to be very autonomous from the Curia; it ought to be above the Curia, above its head, whether he is the secretary of State, as is the case today, or someone else. The Curia should continue to give its own proper service to the Pope with reduced personnel, with a less honorific use of the episcopate, and with internal vigilance constituted by bodies which can act (here, yes) as 'crown councils' to guarantee the Roman Pontiff greater efficiency and more cleanness. It will be the Pope who will set things going on this or that matter, if there are executive jobs to be done, and it will be the senate that gathers loyalty and disloyalty in giving voice to the '*mens papae*' [mind of the Pope]. If the Curia were given permanent 'agency' in the collegial body, this would mean once again sacrificing space to the universalism which is inherent in the Curia. Instead, it would be within the power of the senate, together with the Pope, to take decisions away from the Curia on any matter, and to set up temporary congregations *ad negotiam* [working parties], who will work for a very limited time, be directly answerable to the collegial body and also be able to meet in other places away from Rome, when necessary.

X Conclusion

Perhaps these options will be decided in the near future. Perhaps the technical complications of modifying the Curia (for the matter of the IOR [Vatican Bank] alone, in a few months Francis has set up two commissions and a prelate) will force postponements. Only the future will show how serious these are and what are their consequences. These will be seen by a Catholicism which today is beset by a Pentecostal mood, not only from outside, but in the temptation to become a therapeutic and conservative faith.

Translated by Dinah Livingstone

Notes

1. G. Alberigo, *La Chiesa cattolica ai primi del Cinquecento secondo il 'Libellus ad*

Alberto Melloni

Leonem X' degli eremiti camaldolesi Vincenzo Querini e Tommaso Giustiniani, in Una Gerusalemme toscana sullo sfondo di due giubilei 1500–1525, S. Gensini (ed.), Montaione, 2004, pp. 19–29.
2. *Cf.* G. Martina, *Pio IX (1846–1850)*, Rome, 1974, pp. 81–96.
3. *Cf.* the biography of Paul VI, edited by F. De Giorgi, A. Maffeis & X. Toscani, due out in 2014.
4. G. Miccoli, *In difesa della fede: la chiesa di Giovanni Paolo II e Benedetto XVI*, Milan, 2007.
5. *Cf.* the interview with Walter Kasper in *La Repubblica*, 6 March 2013.
6. A. Riccardi, *Giovanni Paolo II. La biografia*, Cinisello Balsamo, 2010.
7. M. Garzonio, *Il profeta. Vita di Carlo Maria Martini*, Milan, 2012.
8. A. Melloni, *Quel che resta di Dio. Un discorso storico sulle forme della vita cristiana*, Turin, 2013.
9. *Cf. Il tradimento strutturale della fiducia*, R. Ammicht, M. Junker-Kenny & H. Haker (eds), in *Concilium* (2004/3; G. Erlandson–M. Bunson, *Benedict XVI and the Sexual Abuse Crisis: Working for Reform and Renewal*, Huntington, II, 2010.
10. *Cf. La Réforme des Religions. Judaïsme, Christianisme, Islam, Hindouisme*, Mohammed Haddad & Alberto Melloni (eds), Münster, 2007.
11. A. Melloni, '*Ohne eine kirchliche Seele zu haben. Reformprojekte der römischen Kurie und das Zweite Vatikanische Konzil in der Sicht von Eugenio Corecco*', in *Das Zweite Vatikanische Konzil und die Zeichen der Zeit Heute*, P. Hünerman (ed.), Freiburg im Breisgau, 2006, pp. 348–61.
12. C. Theobald, *Le Christianisme comme style*, Paris, 2007.
13. As soon as Francis took up the IOR (Vatican Bank) dossier, the blog of the weekly *Espresso*, which the Italian Church had long rated for its efficacy in attacking Catholics held to be unpopular, launched a denunciation which tried, mistakenly, to intimidate the Pope.
14. On the use of the expression by Congar, *cf.* my 'The System and the Truth in the Diaries of Yves Congar', in *Yves Congar Theologian of the Church*, Gabriel Flynn (ed.), Louvain, Paris & Dudley, 2005, pp. 277–302.
15. *Cf.* the still definitive essay by G. Alberigo, '*Le origini della dottrina sullo Ius Divinum del Cardinalato (1053–1087)*', in *Reformata reformanda, Festgabe für Hubert Jedin zum 17. Juni 1965*, I, Münster, 1965, pp. 39–58.
16. On Dosetti's theses: at the end of 1997 G. Alberigo, in *Coscienza di un secolo*, E. Galavotti (ed.), Bologna, 2013, studied the critical analyses of the Council developed by Dossetti, and in particular: 'A capital failing of the Council: the conciliar Fathers were not in fact aware of the true dimensions and true content of the institutional problem, thus giving up a priori on the chapter *De Reformatione*. The dissenting speeches attacking the Curia reduced everything to a question of personalities, juridical formulae, moral questions and customs, whereas the problem of the Curia is a real theological problem ... It is not a question of discussing whether the Pope ought or not to have helpers (which is a matter course), or about the way in which they should be organized. It is a question of examining the theology of the primacy with regard to its intrinsic, theological nature, in order to know, not the quantity of power that can be shared, but, with whom it is to be shared, and to what extent. Therefore the problem is one of radical reform, which requires a total demobilization of the Curia and its reduction to an extremely slender and agile body for study, control, but very supple control and in most cases only after the event. Without all its machinations attempting to control everything in advance, [the Curia] could become a real organ of planning

and study. As for the normative function, this should obviously be exercised by the Pope himself, or with the participation of the episcopal College, the only synod that truly represents the whole Church in its deepest reality.'

17. In 1967 Paul VI promulgated his reform that came into force the following year. It made the Secretary of State the Pope's prime minister and radicalized the internationalization of personnel. In 1988 John Paul II modified the lower order of the Montinian Curia and re-absorbed the secretariats invented by Pope John into pontifical councils. However, without any formal acts, Pope John had already made the Secretary of State head of the Curia, giving him the function of president of the pre-preparatory and preparatory commission for Vatican II. In 2007, by nominating a helper outside the political dimensions as Secretary of State, Benedict XVI readopted the Pacellian (Pius XII) idea (which left that post vacant from 1945 until his death) of seeing to these dossiers himself.

18. See G. La Bella, *Roma e l'America Latina. Il Resurgimiento cattolico sudamericano*, Rome 2012.

19. A. Melloni, *'L'agenda della chiesa, l'agenda del conclave'*, in *La scelta di Benedetto. Indagine sulla grande rinuncia*, F. De Bortoli (ed.), Milan, 2013, pp. 125–32.

20. H. Fries & K. Rahner, *Einigung der Kirchen – reale Möglichkeit*, Freiburg im Breisgau, 1987.

21. A. Indelicato, *Il sinodo dei vescovi. La collegialità sospesa (1965–1985)*, Bologna, 2008, also for Bertoletti's contribution of, which perhaps Bergoglio was acquainted with.

22. On the day after any papal election, we see in the press the enthusiasm with which the cardinals speak about the action of God, referring to the pre-conclave congregations which are free. *Cf.* A. Melloni, *Il conclave. Storia dell'elezione del papa*, Bologna, 2013.

23. The communiqué reads thus: 'Taking up a suggestion that emerged during the course of the general congregations preceding the conclave, the Holy Father Francis has set up a group of cardinals to advise him on the government of the universal Church and to study a project of revision of the apostolic constitution *Pastor bonus* on the Roman Curia.' There follows a list of names, which include Cardinals Giuseppe Bertello, Francisco Javier Errázuriz Ossa, Oswald Gracias, Reinhard Marx, Laurent Monsengwo Pasinya, Sean Patrick O'Malley and George Pell. It ends with Oscar Andrés Rodríguez Maradiaga 'with office of co-ordinator' and Marcello Semeraro 'with office of secretary'. The first joint meeting of the group was fixed for 1–3 October 2013. Meanwhile the Pope is still in contact with the above-mentioned cardinals. The double agenda is relevant: to draw up a constitutional plan for the revision of the Curia and 'to advise on the government of the universal Church'.

24. The affixed date is 28 September. The text reads: 'After the suggestions that emerged during the course of the general congregations of cardinals before the conclave, it was found appropriate to set up a restricted group of members of the episcopate from different parts of the world, whom the Holy Father can consult either singly or collectively, on particular questions. Since I was elected to the See of Rome, I have had occasion to reflect a number of times on this matter. I believe that such an initiative will be of notable help to carry out the pastoral ministry of the Successor of Peter, with which my brother cardinals have entrusted me. For this reason, on 13 April last, I announced the setting up the above-mentioned group, and indicated at the same time the names of those who had been called to be part of it. Now, after mature reflection, I think it opportune that such a group, through this present chirograph, should be set

up as a 'council of cardinals' with the task of helping me in the government of the universal Church and to study a revision project of the apostolic constitution *Pastor bonus* on the Roman Curia. This will be composed of the same persons previously named, who can be consulted, either as a council or singly, on questions which from time to time I deem to require attention. With respect to the number of members of the said council, I plan to configure it in the way that will prove most adequate. The council will be a further expression of the episcopal communion and a help to the *munus petrinum* [office of Peter], which the episcopate scattered throughout the world can provide.'

25. *Cf. Rappresentata. Mappino a Key Word for Churches and Governance. Proceedings of the San Miniato International Workshop, October 2004*, M. Faggioli & A. Melloni (eds), Münster, 2006, pp. 3–10.

Cognitive Dissonance? Still Minding the Gap between Council and Curia

GERARD MANNION

I Introduction

In this article I examine the dilemma of practices and mind-sets in the Roman Curia that have stood in contrast to directives of Vatican II. I consider the welcome return to the spirit of reform, why it remains necessary, and the complex factors behind the divergence in conciliar and curial perspectives. I also explore some of the most significant areas where the foregoing has been witnessed. I suggest that the theory of cognitive dissonance is a fruitful way of interpreting the divergence between Council and Curia. Issues of ecclesial dialogue, participation and co-responsibility loom large in any such consideration. In particular, questions of collegiality and the lay apostolate point towards a wider divergence in relation to the understanding and practice of magisterium, which in turn indicates even wider and fundamental differences between Vatican II's ecclesiological vision and that which has prevailed in Rome in recent times. A more humble and service-oriented self-understanding of the Curia, coupled with a revisiting of conciliar theory attuned to a twenty-first-century world, could offer great hope of a final implementation of the Council in view of a flourishing future for the Church.

At various stages in the history of the Church, there have been calls for ecclesial reform in 'head and members', the head most often referring, as Congar reminds us, to the Roman Curia rather than to the papacy alone.[1] At Vatican II, it became equally clear that relations between the wider Church and the Roman offices of ecclesial organization required transformation in response to the needs of our times. Pope Paul VI urged that 'everything the Council decreed should be religiously and devoutly observed by all the faithful'.[2] If the Council was so clearly in favour of wide and sweeping reforms, including that of the Curia, why are we still talking about such reforms in the second decade of the twenty-first century? Are there grounds for hope that, this time, reform will be genuine and far-reaching. Pope Paul told the conciliar Fathers that they were responsible for determining the precise details of ecclesial reform in terms of changes in church legislation and discipline, and they should also indicate 'what decisions are required for purifying and rejuvenating the Church's image'.[3] Why then did a very different situation come to pass, and what have been the consequences?

II Curial cognitive dissonance?

To reflect on the actual practices of the Roman Curia in post-conciliar times which stand in conflict with the Council's directives is not simple. It does not mean merely producing a list showing where curial practices have been contrary to the Council's will and directives. There are several reasons to explain the complexity of any such divergence.

First, Pope Paul VI, following his apostolic namesake, tried to be all things to all people when it came to curial reform. In an earlier address to the Curia he had actually assured its members that *they* would be the ones to determine the reform of the body they worked in themselves.[4] So while Paul VI eventually told the Council that some curial reform would indeed take place (in his allocution address on 18 November 1965), and that he would be establishing the synod of bishops, he also disappointed many of his listeners by telling them that no substantial changes to the structure of the Curia were actually required.[5] Furthermore, with some notable exceptions, he also decided that the Roman congregations would actually be responsible for implementing the *conciliar* decrees.[6]

Second, while there are numerous instances where subsequent curial practices have indeed directly thwarted or slowed the pace of reform, and even reversed the will and directives of the Council, an especially significant problem was that the conciliar Fathers deliberately left divisive issues of vital importance for the future of the Church unresolved, or were even reluctantly obliged to do so. Moreover, there are numerous instances where the Fathers, the coordinating bodies (or even Paul VI) also introduced compromises, qualifications and even contradictory elements into the conciliar documents themselves.[7]

Third, the Fathers represented widely differing viewpoints, and the Curia itself was diversified with a variety of voices and perspectives within. However, some voices and perspectives have proved more influential than others, and more progressive voices which did not sit well with the most influential curial actors have usually, sooner or later, found themselves excluded from key decisions and have been kept in the dark on key curial documents, even those that directly concern their own curial dicastery.

Fourth, negative curial activity *vis-à-vis* the Council's reforms and directives has been witnessed in various forms and waves. Some such activity commenced even before the Council itself had even officially begun. Then there are the negative curial activities that countermanded aspects of the Council's spirit and letter of reform during the Council itself, as curial factions and like-minded Fathers became ever more adept at out-manoeuvring the most reform-minded conciliar Fathers and *periti* in the commissions and committees. Such activities rapidly gathered pace towards the end of the Council (for example, during the 'black week' of 14–21 November 1964). Luis Antonio (now Cardinal) Tagle has described *la settimana nera* of the Council, a period when many of the Fathers 'felt that they had approved texts severely weakened by concessions granted in order to win over a defiant minority'.[8] Such activities increased in a marked fashion immediately after the Council's final session. It would appear that these negative voices increasingly claimed the attention of Pope Paul VI.

In fact, the Curia and wider church leadership would become steadily dominated in the post-conciliar years by an ecclesial agenda and programme that could legitimately be described as a veritable road-block of Vatican II in terms of many of its most important reforming principles and teachings.[9] From the late 1960s onwards, Catholics increasingly began to position themselves in different ecclesiological and ecclesial 'camps'. Some embraced and advocated swift change in many areas of church life. Others wished for a slower pace of reform and renewal, while yet others began to perceive the changes being implemented in negative terms and with increasing alarm and fear. These are the divisions that continue to plague the Church to this very day.

A large number of events, church teaching documents, theological perspectives and ecclesial developments have contributed to this state of affairs. One of the most significant factors was the growing influence of the group of theologians who came together to form what became openly known as the *Communio* programme. Their vision and prescription for the future of the Church has gradually transformed ecclesial life, not least of all through their ideas coming to prevail in the Curia and through the attempted imposition throughout the Church of a normative understanding of *Communio* ecclesiology.[10]

We might therefore apply the theory of cognitive dissonance to these ecclesial developments.[11] Strong and influential voices within the Roman Curia and like-minded church leaders and theologians beyond Rome could not reconcile the reforming vision and energy of Vatican II with their own preferred ecclesiological and spiritual world-view.

Slowly but surely, this disturbing experience of cognitive dissonance (the disjuncture between what they believed the Church was like and should continue to be like, what it had taught and should continue to teach; how it was organized, led and governed in the past, and the radically transformed structures, organizations, teachings and governance now being proposed by the majority at Vatican II) would give rise to strategies and reactionary tactics that would prove highly effective. The will of the Council in key areas would be thwarted, key reforms tempered, delayed or over-turned altogether. New bodies and initiatives designed to de-centralize the Church would in fact be utilized to increase Rome's control around the globe. As years turned into decades, even the decrees of Vatican II itself would be deployed against the spirit and reform of the Council.

Revisionist perspectives of what the Council 'really' meant and intended would appear in official pronouncements and documents. A sense of the 'authentic' interpretation of Vatican II would be prioritized over differing perspectives. In time, official discourse about Vatican II would be transformed from being primarily about ecclesial change to being an instrument of affirming ecclesial continuity. In effect, the implementation of the strategy to deal with the disturbing experience of ecclesial cognitive dissonance was so successful that, in a number of important ways, by the beginning of the second decade of the twenty-first century, the Church had effectively moved backwards in time rather than forwards. Many people would behave as if Vatican II had never happened, or at least as if what had happened was very different from what reformers had experienced.

None of this is to suggest that the Curia could be deemed solely responsible for such a reaction to the Council. We should not forget the numerous persons within the Curia both during and since the Council who worked tirelessly to bring Vatican II's vision towards greater fulfilment. However, the voice of those curial actors who opposed much of the Council has proved dominant.

III Curia and Council in greatest contrast

Issues of dialogue, ecclesial participation and co-responsibility provide something like a key to understanding several of the most important challenges and post-conciliar travails vis-à-vis lasting ecclesial reform. In turn, these issues, in themselves, point to the wider challenges concerning the understanding of magisterium and ecclesial governance that have prevailed following the Council. Finally, all these point to a deep dissonance between the spirit and intentions of Vatican II in relation to the understanding of what the Church is, and what should be its aspirations and most pressing tasks for the future, and the very different answers to such questions developed subsequently in parts of Rome and elsewhere. In other words, the most fundamental differences are ecclesiological, both in terms of institutional and organizational self-understanding (that is, socio-political factors), and in terms of theological factors. All in all, the issue of curial reform is both an organizational and a theological question.

a) Dissonance and participation: Collegiality and the lay apostolate

Among the most significant conciliar texts where the theological and organizational components come together in an especially fruitful fashion, are paragraphs 9 and 10 of the Decree on the Pastoral Office of Bishops, *Christus Dominus* (1965). In these texts we see a call for a reorganization of the Curia that is more attentive to the signs of the times. They also highlight the importance of embracing cultural and geographical diversity, particularly the need for a better appreciation in the Curia of the different rites and practices throughout the communion of global churches. There is also a call for an internationalization of the curial personnel, so that they reflect more effectively the universal Church they are called to serve.

There is also an explicit call for the Curia to take heed of the advice of laypeople 'who are outstanding for their virtue, knowledge, and experience. In such a way they will have an appropriate share in church affairs', a call echoed also in proposals for reform of diocesan curias, too (par. 27). The general will of the Council was for the Curia not only to be aware of but to reflect the diversity and particular concerns of the different churches around the world in its personnel and in its day-to-day operations.

For a certain number of conciliar Fathers and curial officials alike, collegiality, witnessed as so effective during Vatican II itself, was the very problem. Much of what the Council said about the role of bishops and particularly collegiality was effectively also a perspective on the role of the Curia and the need for transformations of its structure and operation. The issue of the Curia was present throughout the Council. The reactionary interventions and behind-the-scenes activities of Cardinal Ottaviani are now legendary. But this did not end with the Council's final session. The reforms detailed in *Christus Dominus* would not come to pass as envisioned.

Perhaps one of the greatest disappointments for the majority of Fathers was the eventual 'toning down' of the affirmation of collegiality, through the insertion of a famous *Nota praevia* (a preliminary note) into the Dogmatic Constitution on the Church, *Lumen gentium*.[12] This note, which sought to clarify the notion of collegiality contained in chapter three of the constitution, effectively made clear that the College of Bishops exercises its authority only in so far as the Pope assents to it doing so.

Obviously, the issue of the Synod of Bishops is closely related to the notion of collegiality and to the reform of the Curia in general. This was identified by Bernard Häring as 'perhaps the most crucial structural reform' to follow from the Council.[13] The Council's will concerning the establishment of the synod is detailed in paragraph 5 of *Christus Dominus*.

We now know, alas, that the synod as it stands has been a failure in terms of putting collegiality into practice, and it has become increasingly subordinated to the will and practice of the curial departments, most especially that of the CDF. Häring gives us glimpses of what the conciliar hopes were in relation to the synod, but, alas, it ended up functioning neither as *concilium* nor as *synodos*, in the words of Ludwig Kaufman.[14] For Hans Küng, the synod all too quickly became no more than 'a debating club'.[15]

The outcome, then, is a far cry from the intentions of Vatican II, which wished to see the Curia at the service not simply of the Pope as head of the college of bishops, but of the college, itself, particularly by serving the synod as a representative body of the bishops.[16] Indeed, not only has the synod been undermined as an effective body determining and expressing collegial will, but so, too, have national episcopal conferences. This, again, in contrast to the will of the Council.

The other great question of ecclesial participation here concerns the understanding of the lay apostolate and notions of what would eventually be termed lay ministry. The conciliar vision for the laity[17] has been especially turned upon its head in many important ways. The sense of mutuality and collaboration, the affirmation of the full participation of the laity in the threefold office of Christ, were gradually transformed by a renewed hierarchical and limiting understanding of ministry in the Church. Compare the conciliar decrees, for example, with the 1997 *Instruction on the Collaboration of the Non-ordained Faithful in the Sacred Ministry of Priest*, which bore the signatures of the leading officials from several curial departments.[18] Such a document placed clear limitations on the place and role of the laity in the Church, not least of all in response to developments in some parts of the Church directly inspired by Vatican II.

b) Dissonance and magisterium

To return to the theological questions, which, of course, also have practical and moral implications. Under Paul VI to a certain extent, and increasingly so under John Paul II and Benedict XVI, the Curia has been allowed to assume an ecclesial authority that it does not warrant and should not enjoy. From both a theological and an organizational perspective, parts of the post-conciliar Curia have not served the Church well in its attempts to live out the Gospel in practice. Indeed, there has prevailed in recent times a sense that the Curia's role within the 'Holy See' bestows all the authority and approval of the papacy itself upon all curial actions.

In addition to curial actions and pronouncements that even, at times, appear to have usurped aspects of the authority and/or governance previously deemed the prerogative of the Pope, the Curia in recent times has not only seemed to usurp the function and authority previously deemed proper to the college of bishops, but has done so with regard to the authority, standing and role of the Church's theological community, again as these were understood in the decrees of Vatican II. In fact, the Curia has issued numerous documents that have sought to narrow the remit and freedom of Catholic theologians. The Council envisioned a more collaborative relationship between scholars, bishops and Rome. Instead the sense of the CDF as an organ of inquisition, enforcing a rigid orthodoxy, has dominated far too much of ecclesial life in the post-conciliar decades.

Furthermore, in the words and deeds of curial offices in recent decades we have also seen a 'downgrading' of the importance of conscience, of the *sensus fidelium*, and therefore of the teaching authority of all the People of God.

One obvious example here where the Curia appears to encroach on the rôles and authority of bishops and theological community alike, is the presumption by some curial departments, most notably the CDF, that they can speak more authoritatively on contested theological and moral matters than both the college of bishops and the community of Catholic theologians worldwide. This, at the very least, poses something of a doctrinal chicken-and-egg dilemma. This did not exist at other stages of history, because Rome did not presume to determine the answers to all doctrinal and moral conundrums, but adjudicated or convened synods and councils in order to do so, following the deliberations of other competent authorities throughout the Church, including those of the theological schools. Richard Gaillardetz has observed that the distinction between the Curia's executive and legislative roles has come to be ignored and therefore the curial congregations 'have virtually replaced the college of bishops as the principal legislators in the Church'.[19]

Therefore one way of summarizing all of the tensions and contradictions between curial policy and practice in recent times and the spirit and will of Vatican II is to state that the model of magisterium that has prevailed in the last 40 or so years, and especially in the last 30 years, is in many ways antithetical to what the conciliar Fathers intended for the Church of the late twentieth and twenty-first century.

There are further areas of dissonance between Council and curial actions and policies for which I do not have enough space here. They would include priestly and religious life and formation, relations with other churches, faiths and people of no faith, religious freedom, and communications and the liturgy, among other areas. There is even dissonance between aspects of *Dei verbum*, for example in relation to the necessary development of doctrine and subsequent curial pronouncements. Although *Gaudium et spes* was itself the product of much disagreement during the Council, we can see that a great deal of the spirit and letter of this document has proved especially unpopular among prominent curial voices in the subsequent ecclesial era.

All in all, a spirit of freedom and cooperation prevails throughout most of the conciliar documents; there is also a sense of co-responsibility and due acknowledgment of people and groups within the Church with particular charisms, training and expertise, who should be facilitated in order to allow such gifts to benefit the Church. That also stands in marked contrast to the prevailing attitude in the Curia in post-conciliar and recent times.

The Council's positive engagement with the wider world, and with people of other churches, other faiths and of no faith (in other words its world-affirming attitude) is something that much of the Curia resolutely turned against subsequently and especially in recent decades. A world-renouncing perspective and official ecclesiology in marked contrast to the spirit and letter of the Council prevailed in too many quarters of Rome for all too long.

IV Still waiting on Vatican II

In fact, in spite of the hope and promise of reform, Pope Paul ultimately strengthened and consolidated the Curia and its influence throughout the wider Church. Both John Paul II and Benedict XVI would take this trend even further. Huizing and Walf concur: 'The reorganization of the Curia ... has accentuated its rôle as the executive body of the Pope even more'.[20]

At the very time that episcopal collegiality was supposed to become the key to ecclesial leadership, teaching and governance, Vatican II's vision for the future was being undermined. Not only did members of the Curia set about limiting what conciliar reforms they could, but did so at the very same time when an alternative, even a 'competing advisory body to the Pope'.[21] had been established in the form of the synod (a body no less under the full control of the Pope himself and subject to any changes he wished to make), and there was an enormous increase in the very number of people working in the Curia, from 1322 in 1961 to 3146 in 1977.[22]

Admittedly, many curial posts were internationalized in certain congregations and offices. However, the sense of 'business as usual' for the Curia in fact become 'business is booming' by the mid-1970s and beyond. Yet many of those international additions to the Curia became more 'Roman' than the natives. The curial grip on the appointment of bishops worldwide, in addition to appointments to curial bodies and even the College of Cardinals, has further widened the gap between Vatican II and the *Curia Romana*.

In keeping with the theme of ecclesial cognitive dissonance, one might actually say that, instead of Vatican II's decrees leading directly to a wholesale reform of the Roman Curia, many individuals in the Roman Curia set about 'reforming' the spirit and letter of much of Vatican II. This was not the first time in history that a Council's will had been changed in Rome.

Yet there is a great irony in all this. Citing W. Foerster's study of the Modernist crisis, Yves Congar reminds us that when 'a certain kind' of person is recruited for the Church's central administration, this ends up isolating papal power, rather than reinforcing it.[23] Congar had in mind the conservative, 'safe' type of appointment, those who emphasize fidelity and tradition alone, those who 'don't cause problems' or surprises and who 'don't take any risks'. What effectively happens is that a barrier is built up between the administration and the wider Church, and the centre becomes a 'party'.[24] Congar's words served as a warning that has yet to be heeded in Rome. Huizing and Walf offer a similar perspective,[25] as does Lécuyer: 'As soon as the Curia becomes self-centred, thinks that it is infallible and can ignore what all the other faithful feel or think, it will be unfaithful to the Spirit and serve the Pope in the worst possible way by isolating him and cutting his indispensable contact with the whole People of God', that People of God whom *Lumen gentium* par. 12 makes clear penetrate the faith ever more deeply with their insights and discern its lived expression.[26]

Vatican II's sense of the Church as 'People of God' has been supplanted by a normative emphasis upon communion with Rome, i.e. the relation to the centre is primary, with all the centralized control and uniformity in doctrine, practice and viewpoint that this entails.

Nobody need fear a reform of the Curia. The objections to any such reform that were raised at the Council, and have been raised since then, for instance that it would weaken the papacy and its authority throughout the Church, because the Curia serves the Pope first and foremost, simply do not hold. In fact, 'The papacy, which possesses a unique and inalienable charisma of community, would be freer to develop its world mission if it were to be liberated from a too centralized structure'[27] Co-responsibility is the lasting legacy of the Council, and the key to a flourishing future for the Church. The *sine qua non* of the Church truly embracing collective responsibility is wide-reaching reform of the Curia. It is time for change.

Indeed, it is time for a return to considerations of forms of conciliar theory for that, in a twenty-first century form, could help deliver each and every one of the desires for ecclesial dialogue, participation and co-responsibility that were so dear to the leading voices at Vatican II. Simone Weil speaks of a need 'To give up our imaginary position as the centre, to renounce it, not only intellectually but in the imaginative part of our soul, that means to awaken to what is real and eternal, to see the true light and hear the true silence. A transformation then takes place at the very roots of our sensibility'.[28] Can the Curia at last be reformed, so that it no longer perceives itself as the most important part of the Church but rather learns to behave as though it were the least and therefore truly fulfils its own vocation as the servant of the servant of the servants of God, of the successors of the other apostles, and therefore of the whole People of God?

Notes

1. Yves Congar, *True and False Reform in the Church*, tr. Paul Philibert, Collegeville, 2011, p. 361. A point echoed in Bernard Häring, *Road to Renewal: Perspectives of Vatican II*, New York, 1966, p. 17.
2. In his apostolic letter *In Spiritu Sancto*, which was read out at the 8 December 1965 closing ceremony, AAS IV/7, p. 885, cited in John O'Malley, *What Happened at Vatican II*, Cambridge, MA., 2008, p. 289.
3. *Ecclesiam suam* (6 August 1964), paragraph 44. Congar included sections of this encyclical as Appendix III to his *True and False Reform*.
4. Address of 21 September 1963, AAS II/1, pp. 49–56 at 54, cited in O'Malley, *What Happened at Vatican II*, p. 171. See also: 'Editorial' in Peter Huizing & Knut Walf (eds), *The Roman Curia and the Communion of Churches*, Concilium 127 (1979/7), New York, vii–xv at viii. Paul's decision was confirmed in the 1967 Apostolic Constitution *Regimini ecclesiae universae*, http://www.vatican.va/holy_father/paul_vi/apost_constitutions/documents/hf_p-vi_apc_19670815_regimini-ecclesiae-universae_it.html.
5. *AAS* IV/6, pp. 689–95.
6. O'Malley, *What Happened at Vatican II*, p. 283.
7. On conciliar 'unfinished business', see, for example, Paul Lakeland's excellent recent study, *A Council that will Never End*, Collegeville, 2013.
8. Luis Antonio G. Tagle, in Giuseppe Alberigo & Joseph A. Komonchak (eds), *History of Vatican II*, Maryknoll, NY & Leuven,1995–2005, vol. IV, p. 387.
9. A further complication is that the implementation of some conciliar reforms actually went much further than what was envisioned at the Council itself, for example the use of the vernacular in the liturgy.
10. See Joseph Ratzinger, 'Communio – Ein Programm', *Internationale Katholische Zeitschrift* 21 (1992), pp. 454–63 (tr., Peter Casarella, 'Communio: A Program', *Communio: International Review*, vol. 19, 3 (1992), pp. 436–49. *Cf.* Gerard Mannion, *Ecclesiology and Postmodernity: Questions for the Church in Our Times*, Collegeville, Minn., 2007, esp. chapters 2–4, and Lieven Boeve & Gerard Mannion (eds), *The Ratzinger Reader*, New York & London, 2010, esp. ch. 3, esp. 113–8, which introduces and contains an abridged version of Ratzinger's account of the Communio programme.
11. The classic text is Leon Festinger's *When Prophecy Fails: A Social and Psychological Study of a Modern Group That Predicted the Destruction of the World*, New York, 1956. One of the first and most famous authors to apply this theory to biblical studies defines the theory thus: cognitive dissonance, 'seeks to analyze response to disconfirmations of attitudes, beliefs or expectations brought about by counter-information or experience. Discomforting evidence is said to produce dissonance among individuals or groups. Attempts are made to deny such disconfirmation or to reinterpret either the dissonant information or the original set of beliefs in order to restore consonance between it and reality. Dissonance resolution is a psychological mechanism which brackets unpleasant

truths and protects individuals or groups from the necessity of having to change the belief system', Robert P. Carroll, 'Dissonance, Cognitive', in Alan Richardson & John Bowden, *A New Dictionary of Christian Theology*, London, 1983, pp. 158–9.
12. Although the nota was actually added to the text as an appendix.
13. Häring, *Road to Renewal*, op. cit., p. 18.
14. 'Synods of Bishops: Neither '"concilium" nor "synodos"' in J. Provost & K. Walf (eds), 'Collegiality put to the Test', *Concilium* (1990/4), pp. 67–78.
15. Hans Küng, *Disputed Truth: Memoirs, vol. II*, London & New York, 2008, p. 23.
16. Thereby entailing that the supreme authority in the Church is exercised collegially rather than personally, Lécuyer, 'Place of the Roman Curia...', p. 9.
17. Most explicitly seen in *Apostolicam actuositatem* but witnessed throughout multiple conciliar documents also, not least of all, *Gaudium et spes*.
18. http://www.vatican.va/roman_curia/pontifical_councils/laity/documents/rc_con_interdic_doc_15081997_en.html.
19. Gaillardetz, *Teaching with Authority*, op. cit., p. 287.
20. Huizing & Walf, 'Editorial', *op. cit.*, p.viii.
21. *Ibid.*, viii (emphasis added).
22. *Ibid.*, ix.
23. Yves Congar, True and False Reform, *op. cit.*, p. 264, citing W. Foerster, *Autorité et Liberté*, tr., Lausanne, 1920, pp. 138–48.
24. Ibid., p. 264.
25. Huizing & Walf, 'Editorial', *op. cit.*, p. xiv.
26. Lécuyer, 'Place of the Roman Curia...', *op. cit.*, p. 7.
27. Huizing & Walf, 'Editorial', *op. cit.*, p. xiv.
28. Simone Weil, *Waiting for God*, New York, p. 159.

Roman Primacy, Communion between Churches, and Communion between Bishops

HERVÉ LEGRAND

I Introduction

The reform of the Roman Curia as announced by Pope Francis will be more than simply managerial. It is to be accompanied by an as yet undefined reassertion of collegiality. The Pope has shunned self-referentiality and clericalism, and advocates an ecclesiology of communion to deepen the links between bishops and the faithful (more synodality) and, accordingly, between bishops from the same region (more collegiality). He sees his primacy as rooted in his Roman episcopate, and as serving the communion of churches (note the plural). The Curia would no longer be above the bishops, but would be before them, as it were, and accountable to them at the same time as to the Pope. This should simultaneously correct the current universal notion of the episcopal college, to which a bishop could belong in a personal capacity, and the passivity of local churches without any say in the choice of their pastors.

During the recent pre-conclave, the cardinals favoured reforming the Curia and approved an effective collegiality. In this context, Cardinal Bergoglio wanted 'to elucidate possible reforms', and on six occasions called in question 'the self-referentiality of the Church, a source of sickness in ecclesial institutions'. He referred four times to the importance of the 'geographical and existential outskirts' when disavowing the current centralization. He stressed all this to ensure that the Church 'gets out of itself' in order to evangelize.[1] Far from resorting to the distinction between the Church *ad intra* and the Church *ad extra*, he testified, in his first words and decisions as Pope, to his keen

63

awareness of the link between the institutional life of the Church and its capability of living the Gospel and bearing witness to it.

II The reforms of Curia, collegiality and papacy are interconnected

Of their very nature, the reforms envisaged will necessarily prove to be systematic. Even at the time of the vote in favour of collegiality, the future Cardinal Yves Congar remarked: 'Vatican II counterbalanced Vatican I with a majority that never went below 87 per cent and thus gave the episcopate more significance and initiative than the actual governance of the Church, which is now dominated by a certain exercise of the papal primacy, and constitutes the curial and Roman centralized system', which is 'followed by all those other churches which acknowledge the absolutist and monarchical power of the papacy'.[2]

Fifty years later, Pope Francis begins by reforming the Curia, without placing it at the centre of his proposal, which aims to intensify the ecclesial communion between the bishop and his people, between local churches, between their bishops, and between them and the Bishop of Rome, at one and the same time. To be successful, the adjustments to what we might call 'ecclesiological trajectories' that will be required in order to achieve this aim will have to be transposed into canon law and management. I cannot discuss these canonical and managerial strategies in detail, but I shall try to analyze the associated complex of new theological problems in relation to the last two pontificates.

III Collegiality depends on the status of local churches

People found the first gesture of Pope Francis surprising. But it was in line with his ecclesiology and was never improvised. Instead of immediately giving his initial blessing to people and the world, the first thing he did, against all expectation, was to ask the faithful to pray for him. In keeping with the emphasis on the People of God of *Lumen gentium* (LG: The Dogmatic Constitution on the Church),[3] he located the bishop in the Church and the Church in the bishop, in accordance with St Cyprian and St Augustine,[4] thus challenging a clericalism which he also firmly rejected in his address to the CELAM leadership (Council of Bishops' Conferences of Latin America and the Caribbean).[5] Before the same bishops, he stressed the fact that 'We [bishops] are very behind in including the faithful' (that is, with regard to synodality). For Francis, synodality should accompany the new emphasis on collegiality. The Vatican II guidelines pointing in this direction were discarded by the 1983 Code, which in fact attributed to all holders of authority (the Pope, bishops and parish priests, at their level) a sovereign exercise of the powers of their office, without interference from the other faithful or their peers. Accordingly, the current mode of government, in spite of so many councils, is still generally absolutist in character,[6] with regrettable consequences,[7] both pastoral and ecumenical.[8] If this trajectory, which has distorted the conception of collegiality and of primacy, is not adjusted, the only result of reforms will be to improve the current management of the Church.

IV Collegiality and the status of dioceses

The affirmation that 'particular churches ... are constituted after the model of the universal Church', and that 'it is in these and formed out of them that the one and unique Catholic Church exists' (LG 23), will stay an empty formula as long as dioceses cannot express themselves in the communion of churches, and as long as the bishop is located only above his diocese and over against it. Reactivation of the various existing councils, as Pope Francis has requested, will constitute a first step towards the revaluation of the diocesan synod, which is more significant as the very place of expression of the People of God, because it brings together bishop, clergy, men and women religious, and laity. At present, however, it is forbidden to pronounce even a wish that does not conform to the law in force.[9] How can we reinforce the diocesan synod? By fixing the frequency of its meetings and by extending its prerogatives. It could, for example, help to prepare a list of possible bishops in conjunction with the priests' council, another important organ of the local church.

Other arrangements could result in the mutual inclusion of the bishop and his church. They might include making his consecration at the centre of his flock mandatory; giving his reception greater meaning than today; requiring him to give an annual account of his ministry to a general assembly of diocesan councils, and to the synod on his convocation. As far as auxiliary or coadjutor bishops are concerned, they should be associated with the see and not receive the title of some long-vanished church.

If nothing is done to restore the dioceses' status as constitutive elements of the communion of churches, they will continue to deteriorate to the level of administrative areas of the universal Church, which is exactly what they have become in the post-conciliar legal system, which has included a considerable number of non-diocesan constituencies among them.[10] One effect of this development is to be found in the *Dizionario di Ecclesiologia* published in Rome in 2011, which has three entries for 'ecclesial constituencies', but none for 'diocese', which is not to be found anywhere in the final analytical index.[11] This is very odd, since without dioceses possessed of their rights and initiatives we cannot arrive at a true notion of what a bishop, a college of bishops, or an ecclesial communion in the sense of a communion or community of churches (*communio ecclesiarum*) might mean. But surely that is an essential condition of the theological authenticity and acceptability of the suggested reforms. After all, as Ratzinger reminds us, 'The one unique Church is constructed on the basis of numerous local churches'.[12]

V An episcopal college for the heads of local churches

By always presenting himself as the Bishop of the local church of Rome, Pope Francis may be said to propose the adjustment of a second trajectory. In stressing the fact that he is the Bishop of Rome, he underlines the link between the bishop and his church, and revalues the communion of the Church as the communion of churches (in the plural), mediated by the college of their bishops. In this way he reverses the universalist and individualist conception of the episcopate of *Apostolos suos*, which teaches that 'the college of bishops as an essential element of the universal Church is a reality preceding the fact of presiding over a church', because 'as is generally evident, there are numerous bishops who are not at the head of a church': as is the case with 48 per cent of them.[13] But what does it mean to belong to the college in a personal capacity? By multiplying the number of absolute consecrations, the college ceases to be the ordinary channel of the communion of churches, which is already the case of the law that specifies that the college is always dependent on its head, even though the head is under no obligation to collaborate with the college.[14]

Similarly, the universalist interpretation of the episcopate reduces to almost nothing the forms of regional collegiality provided for by LG 23, which introduced bishops' conferences, and suggested that they might be in some way analogous to the patriarchates of the older Church. *Apostolos suos* makes them creations of the Holy See, which institutes them and determines their powers (No. 13). According to No. 20, 'to be legitimate and to be incumbent on different bishops [the pastoral decisions] of the conference require the intervention of the supreme Authority of the Church, which, by universal law or by special mandates, entrusts specific questions to the deliberation of the episcopal conference'.

This same *motu proprio* removes from bishops' conferences the authentic magisterium which can. 753 acknowledged that they possessed, unless they are unanimous.[15] 'Above all they will ensure that they follow the magisterium of the universal Church and make it known opportunely to the people entrusted to them' (No. 21). In short, they will relay the teaching of the Holy See,[16] even though the last paragraph of LG 23 expected them to contribute to the 'catholicity of the undivided Church' and to its inculturation.[17]

When disconnected from the communion of local churches, and when interpreted in a universalist sense, collegiality is effective only in the context of ecumenical councils exclusively convoked by popes (there were three centuries between Trent and Vatican I); in other words, collegiality does not operate at this level. Nor does it operate at the regional level, although the canonical provision in this regard could easily be changed.

VI A proposal

Many spurious problems would disappear, if the everyday government of the universal Church were no longer attributed to the Pope (it is not required by the teachings of Vatican I), and if there were no call for the college to participate in specific functions of the primacy, which would not be shared. Josef Ratzinger's proposal that 'in the not too distant future, the churches of Asia and Africa should become the equivalent of patriarchates, under this designation or some other',[18] would be much easier to implement since we already have (like stepping-stones to the eventual achievement, as it were) continental councils associated with bishops' conferences (CELAM, CCEE, FABC and so on). Their size would protect them from the drawbacks inherent in the national dimension of the current bishops' conferences,[19] which nevertheless 'constitute a legitimate version of the collegial element in the constitution of the Church'.[20] The reserve system could be varied in accordance with the different nature of regional churches. The Eastern Catholic churches already constitute an example of any such procedure, which would avoid the foreseeable dangers of slippage. In fact we cannot credit decentralization with all the virtues formerly attributed to centralization. We need more sensitive criteria.

VII The Roman primacy and a communion of churches

As we know, Pope Francis has formally and firmly criticized the notion of a 'self-referential' Church. He is held to wish to discard the emphasis placed by John Paul II and Benedict XVI on 'the chronological and ontological precedence of the universal Church over particular churches,' and on 'the maternity of the universal Church in respect of individual churches'.[21] Rather than wishing to change the wording of LG 23 *'in quibus et ex quibus'* ('it is in these and formed out of them that the one and unique Catholic Church exists'),[22] Francis, concerned to endorse the 'peripheries', will abstain from presenting the Roman Church as the mother of all the churches, and will behave towards them as if with sisters.[23] He will keep his distance from a maximalist interpretation of Vatican I. Instead he will concentrate on revivifying the communion of churches in the communion of the Church.

VIII Vatican I did not establish centralized church government

The 1983 Code expresses the idea of the everyday governance of the Catholic Church as a matter for the Pope and the Curia.[24] This is the current situation. But this state of affairs is not derived from the definitions of Vatican I. They exclude the transfer of the Pope's prerogatives to the Curia (in the language of 1870 these are non-transferable personal privileges). Moreover, they are not intended to be exercised on a daily basis. This is obvious in the case of infallibility, which emerges from the explanations given to the Fathers before they vote. Ordinary power means that it is complementary to the office, and not habitual or daily.[25] Direct power means that the Pope has no need of any intermediary.[26] This power is full and supreme, for otherwise the primacy would not be an ultimate instance of judgement, but we cannot derive its everyday use from its extension. Furthermore, this power is not in competition with the power of the episcopate. The Pope has not become the bishop of the bishops and of all the faithful, or 'the bishop of the Catholic Church'.[27] When Pius IX approved the response to Bismarck of the German bishops' conference 'to the full extent of his apostolic authority', he confirmed this point as clearly as might be desired.[28] Ratzinger offers a synthesis of common doctrine: 'The current centralization of the Catholic Church is not derived from the Petrine commission, but from the conflation of this office and the patriarchal duty which devolves on the Bishop of Rome [in the West]. The single ecclesiastical law, the single liturgy, the single attribution, by the Roman centre, of episcopal sees – none of these things is necessarily part of the primacy as such'.[29]

We may conclude that there is considerable doctrinal freedom to allow institutions to develop, and especially the present subordination of bishops to the Pope.

IX The subordination of diocesan bishops more traditional than theological

The pre-conciliar centralization, which is surprising in so many respects,[30] has reasserted itself. For example, wishing to know if he could allow young girls to serve Mass like their brothers, a German priest asked the Holy See what he should do in this respect. Instead of referring him to his vicar-general, to his bishop, or to his bishops' conference, two curial dicasteries resolved the problem, in four or five stages, by reference to universal norms.[31] In yet another instance, an Indonesian bishop discovered that bishops' conferences had to submit their liturgical translations 'to Rome for approval by people who neither speak nor understand our languages'.[32]

The envisaged reforms could be inspired by the secular principle of subsidiarity,[33] but they are more likely to resort to the official theology of the episcopate. According to the magisterium of Pius XII, repeated in three encyclicals, the Pope receives the fullness of ecclesiastical power in order to communicate it to the bishops subsequently,[34] but the teaching of the last ecumenical Council is that the bishops receive their charge to govern directly from Christ, in their consecration (LG 26), in order to 'exercise their pastoral office over the portion of the People of God assigned to them, not over other churches or the Church universal' (LG 23 and 28), and it requires us to see them as 'vicars and legates of Christ' and not as vicars of the Roman pontiff ('nor are they to be regarded as vicars of the Roman pontiff; for they exercise the power which they possess in their own right and are called in the truest sense of the term prelates of the people whom they govern' (LG 27). Yet, in the legislation approved by

John Paul II, the status of diocesan bishop in regard to the Pope is legally equivalent to that of a vicar-general in regard to his bishop, and in that legislation he even appears as an 'executive officer of the pope'.[35] Even without Vatican II, a development of this kind would have to be revised, mainly by reform, since the episcopate is established by divine right ('the bishops, inasmuch as they are the successors of the apostles, receive from the Lord, to whom all power is given in heaven and on earth, the mission of teaching all peoples', LG 24).

X No doctrinal objections to the institutional reforms envisaged

According to LG 8, the practice of ecclesiology should be multidisciplinary,[36] especially when dealing specifically with institutions. I shall restrict myself here to some theological reflections not on what is desirable but on what is permissible.

In fact the Curia has been reinforced since Vatican II. The 1983 Code and the Constitution *Pastor bonus* (1988) confirmed it as the direct instrument of the Pope[37] for government of the universal Church. It even exercises a kind of magisterium,[38] although papal teaching has never been inspired in that way.[39] It has scarcely improved its tasks of information and coordination[40] and does not work collegially. Its procedures are more legal and bureaucratic. Since Pope Francis does not want to favour an 'administrative' and 'controlling' Church (his address to CELAM), there will have to be a change of mindset before his reform is completed.

In canonical terms, there seems no reason why the Curia should not operate as a service of the Pope and of diocesan bishops, and no longer of the Pope alone. Symbolically, this would reduce the 'self-referentiality' deplored by Pope Francis and be a suasion for the Curia to give a regular account of its management to some body acting for the pope and representatives of the episcopate (possibly appointed by the Synod of bishops, and independent of the Curia). This would make it subject to evaluation, like any modern administration. Then the direct supervision of the curial administration could be entrusted to a kind of restricted consistory that would also advise the Pope on the diverse tasks associated with the primacy. He would no longer make routine decisions on his own, and would be released from the paradoxical isolation of the presiding figure of the communion of churches.[41] That would be a start to implementing Ratzinger's proposal to dissociate the Petrine primacy from patriarchal duties.

Accordingly, there could be a beneficial revaluation of John Paul II's systematic linking of the offices of the Curia with systematic consecration. The Curia of Pius XII comprised no more than 17 bishops, including cardinals,[42] whereas there are over 80 today. This would get rid of the confusion between the tasks of the primacy and those of the college of bishops. The curial officials would exercise their authentic function as assistants to the primate, and not as also exercising the magisterium in a form of permanent synod without due status. A reform of this kind would also reduce the amount of careerism that Pope Francis has so often deplored.

XI Election of bishops

Since 1917, the choice of bishops has been subject to the adage 'the Roman pontiff freely nominates them' (present can. 327, paragraph 2), which has transformed the former norm into a 'papal concession' (paragraph 3). The adverb 'freely' is very important because, now as in the past, the interests of too many political powers and pressure groups are involved here. It will be important to make sure that the Pope has the last word in this area, while introducing the desired empirical and theological reforms.

In practice, the Pope cannot know the 200 bishops whom he appoints each year and can take only major dioceses into consideration. Two disadvantages have been flagged up here: some nuncios restrict their enquiries to too limited circles,[43] the higher authorities can ignore their advice.[44] An exchange on the selection criteria between bishops' conferences and the Roman congregations concerned would be beneficial. Since the projected reforms are intended to reinforce the meaning of ecclesial communion and common responsibility in local churches, it would be appropriate to prevent bishops keeping the profile of high civil administrators appointed and removed by a central administration, at least by allowing consultation with the local church.[45] Of course we could go further, for, after all, the elections of bishops traditionally express communion between churches,[46] and were generally permissible until 1917.[47] In 1829, outside the Papal States, the Pope appointed only 24 bishops to sees located in the Russian and Ottoman empires.

XII The synod of bishops and the pope

This synod is strictly an advisory council for the pope and not a collegial authority.[48] According to can. 342–8, it can determine neither its composition[49], nor the frequency of its meetings, nor its agenda, and it is not entitled to publish its conclusions under its own auspices. Even if it were reformed, its machinery is too cumbersome to help to bring about the desired collegiality of the cardinals. Its function will probably be re-examined in the context of an overall reform.

XIII The college of cardinals

The college of living cardinals should keep its function as the electoral body of the Bishop of Rome, the reason for the subterfuge by which its members are integrated with the Roman clergy. We have to ask why this election should have anything to do with the college of bishops,[50] precisely when the Church of Rome is rediscovering its function as a local church too. The customary presence of bishops from major sees in the electoral body ensures that it has certain qualities required at its heart, and enables it to assume the *comprobatio* function that goes back to the bishops of the large sees of Antiquity who were entitled to decide the Roman election.[51] But what is the sense of treating honorary cardinals as bishops?[52]

XIV Nuncios and the Vatican State

Pope Francis has already addressed the nuncios in warm tones. He sees them more as priests than as bishops.[53] He confirms their rôle in episcopal nominations.[54] Will their larger function, and that of the Vatican State, which is no more than closely associated, be rethought[55] If the Pope refuses to live in the apostolic Palace, out of fear of a 'worldliness' which he finds objectable, he should live his position as head of State with the same reticence. He is surely the sole bishop to live extraterritorially in relation to his diocese.

XV A primacy in the service of a community of churches

Reforming the Curia as a way of governance that is now inappropriate and on its last legs also means renewing the papacy. If we interpret the definitions of Vatican I correctly, they will not be an obstacle here. The reform will happen once we are rid of a canonical culture that seems so necessary at present when the law has been severed from its theological and traditional roots.[56]

Of course the intention is not to reduce the papacy to the level of a vague centre of communion. How can we celebrate ecumenical councils without a universal primacy?[57] How can we support gospel freedom in the face of totalitarian regimes that promote national and 'patriotic' churches?[58] How are we to offer a counterweight to ethnic and nationalist tensions to which local churches are liable to succumb? The primacy can also stimulate their pastoral work, as with the World Youth Days launched by John Paul II. As far as discipline is concerned, regional churches cannot always control their conflicts or correct abuses without reference to a primacy of some kind. We are brought back to the primacy of regulating exchanges at the heart of communion. Theologically, of course, all local churches are equal, but they have never had, and still do not enjoy, the same financial and theological resources, or the same prestige. Of its charity, a presiding Church can exercise a vigilance which ensures that poor churches are not unduly subject to the dominance of rich churches. Relieved of its self-reference, of the cult of personality practised by some popes, and of appeals to its innate sovereignty, the primacy could be of authentic service to the communion of churches, which is its aim as sought for by John Paul II and Benedict XVI in confirming 'the irreversible ecumenical commitment of the Catholic Church'.

But Catholics are not attached to the primacy of Peter and to its improved functioning because of any eventual practical benefits that it might afford. They favour it because they believe that it is a gift to the Church intended to serve communion between all churches. Surely that end can be achieved only if we already experience the Petrine primacy in that very sense among ourselves now.

Translated by Felicity Leng

Notes

1. These quotations come from his speech to the pre-conclave published in *La Documentation Catholique* 110 (2013), p. 369.
2. Yves Congar, *Le concile au jour le jour. Troisième session*, Paris, 1964, pp. 44, 37 and *ibid.*, 1963, p.18.
3. The practice of *Lumen gentium*, the Dogmatic Constitution on the Church (referred to hereinafter as LG), in treating the people of God before the episcopate is theologically

decisive, but has never been translated into canon law. The extension of the 'right of association' of the laity in the 1983 Code of Canon Law is borrowed from a concept of modern secular law and does not express any rights of communion (*iura communionis*). What the great Lutheran canonist U. Stutz said in 1917 still applies to the 1983 Code: 'The Catholic Church is the church of the clergy and its law almost without exception is a right of the clergy, one in which lay-people have no civil rights but only those extended to protected foreign residents', *Der Geist des* Codex iuris canonici (*Kirchenrechtliche Abhandlungen*, pp. 92–3), Stuttgart, 1918, pp. 83–8.

4. LG 32 cites St Augustine: 'What I am for you, terrifies me; what I am with you consoles me. For I am your bishop; but with you I am a Christian. The former is a title of duty; the latter, one of grace. The former is a danger; the latter, salvation', *Sermon* 340, 1; *PL* (*Patrologia Latina*) 38, 1483. For St Cyprian, *cf.* Letter 66, 8.

5. Five times in five lines he inveighs against 'clericalism, very much a temptation of the moment', *Speech to the CELAM Coordination Committee* in Rio (28 July 2013).

6. Absolutism is defined as the régime in which the individual who exerts the power attached to his or her person, concentrating all powers in his or her hands, governs without any external control over himself or herself (which does not merely mean arbitrary control).

7. For the historian S. Coutinho (Brazil): 'During the last 25 years, we have witnessed an intensive imposition of clericalization and verticalization in the Church. Canon law has acquired great importance in the training of priests, and there has been greater emphasis on obedience ... to the norms of canon law to the detriment of the paths of evangelization ... Consequently, a young priest's sensitivity is more aesthetic and disciplinary than ethical and pastoral ... Pastoral councils tend to ratify the parish priest's decision', *Il Regno* 68, 2013, p. 88.

8. Melanchthon is typical of the Reformers in citing the statements of the Gospel when challenging the *Nichthinterfragbarkeit*, the irrefragable nature, of hierarchical decisions: 'Perhaps our enemies would like the Church to be a monarchy ... in which the Roman pontiff exercises a power that no one has the right to discuss or judge ... However, we have no right to assign to pontiffs alone promises that have been made to the whole Church'. More recently, the Faith and Order Commission Report on baptism, Eucharist and ministry of the World Council of Churches (signed by Catholics) emphasized the fact that the ministers 'are linked to the faithful in interdependence and reciprocity' (*cf.* BEM No. 6).

9. *Cf.* the *Instructio de synodis agendis*, IV, 4, *Acta Apostolicae Sedis* (hereinafter referred to as *AAS*) 89 (1997), pp. 706–27.

10. John Paul II endowed the diocese with an equivalence in law for all ecclesiastical territorial circumscriptions after the Vicariate for the armed forces. Bishops have also been appointed to head the personal prelature, the personal apostolic administration, and, under Benedict XVI, the Ordinariate for former Anglicans.

11. Edited by G. Calabrese, P. Goyret & O.F. Piazza, Rome, 2010. The article 'Chiesa local' is excellent but does not cover the diocese specifically.

12. J. Ratzinger, *The New People of God* (*cf. Le nouveau peuple de Dieu*, Paris, 1970, p. 124).

13. The statement is exact (*cf. Annuario Pontificio* 2013, p. 1140), but the interpretation uncertain. When Pius IX asked if he should summon these bishops to attend Vatican I, the ad hoc Commission replied 'not that he should but that he could', *cf.* Mansi 49, pp. 492–3.

14. Canon 337, paragraph 3, is clear: 'It belongs to the Roman pontiff, according to the needs of the Church, to choose and promote the forms in accordance with which the

college of bishops will carry out its duties with regard to the whole Church'.
15. N. IV, art.12. A unique requirement of unanimity in applicable law.
16. The *recognitio* is to ensure that 'the doctrinal response [of the bishops] does not prejudice interventions of the universal magisterium, but rather is a preparation for them' (No. 22). Consultation of the *Insegnamenti* of John Paul II shows that this 'magisterium' can average over 5000 pages a year (5634 pages in 1982), and even 7410 pages in 1988.
17. 'A discipline, a proper liturgical use, and a theological and spiritual heritage' are mentioned. The term 'inculturation', a later usage, does not appear there.
18. *Cf.* J. Ratzinger, *The New People of God* (*cf. Le nouveau peuple...op. cit.*, pp. 68–9). The idea is repeated there twice.
19. Can. 448, paragraph 1, stipulates that normally they should be national.
20. *Ibid.*, pp. 125–6.
21. This formulation of *Apostolos suos* comes from *Communionis notio*, *AAS 85* (1993), pp. 838–50.
22. *Communionis notio* 9 wished to correct this expression by stating that it was inseparable from the 'phrase, the Churches in and from the Church', AAS 85 (1993), p. 843.
23. The secret letter of the SCDF to all Catholic bishops exclusively identifies the Church of the Roman communion with the universal Church that will be the mother of other Churches. This kind of self-referential attitude makes the schism with the East worse, because, according to Nicetas of Nicodemia, 'We do not refuse the Roman Church the primacy among her sisters', *PL* 118, 1217, and Patriarch John X Camateros replied to Innocent III: 'Where do you find Christ saying in the Holy Scriptures that the Roman Church is a universal mother? ... The Roman Church has the leading position among sisters, equal in dignity, born of the same Father', *PL* 214, 757. Nor does the bull *Laetentur coeli* of the Council of Florence conceive of the Latin Church as the Church abandoned by the Greeks. See H. Legrand, 'La théologie des Églises sœurs', *Revue des sciences philosophiques et théologiques 88* (2004), pp. 461–96.
24. *Cf.* can. 350, paragraph 1: *cura cotidiana universae ecclesiae.*
25. Mansi 52, 1105.
26. *Ibid.*
27. The term 'bishop of the Catholic Church', which Paul VI used to promulgate the Acts of Vatican II, repeats the designation which enabled the popes of the IV and V centuries to distinguish themselves from the other (rival) bishops in the same city, by describing themselves as belonging to the Catholic Church of Rome; on this point see H. Marot, 'Note sur l'expression *Episcopus catholicae ecclesiae*', *Irénikon* 37 (1964), pp. 221–6.
28. *Cf.* Denzinger-Hünermann, Nos. 1132–7.
29. *Le nouveau peuple ..., op. cit.*, p. 68.
30. Even in 1963 a Catholic bishop could not, of his own right, allow a parish priest to celebrate twice on Sunday, without permission from the pope, to be renewed every five years.
31. The question was discussed in 1992, then in 1994, *cf. AAS* 86, 1994, pp. 541–2; with further clarification, *cf.* the *Letter to the Presidents* of the bishops' conferences on liturgical functions carried out by lay-people, *Notitiae* 30 (1994), pp. 333–5, 346–8; and lastly the *Letter to a Bishop, Notitiae* 38 (2002), pp. 49–51.
32. Bishop Hadisumarta, *Origins*, 7 May 1998, pp. 773–4. This duty was re-enforced in 2001, *cf. Liturgiam Authenticam*, No. 80: 'It is an absolute necessary act of government', in the absence of which an act of the episcopal conference would be devoid of all legal value', *AAS 93* (2001), p. 685.
33. On this concept derived from the Church's social teaching, see J. A. Komonchak, 'Le

principe de subsidiarité et sa pertinence ecclésiologique', in H. Legrand (*et al.*), *Les Conférences épiscopales. Théologie, statut canonique, avenir* (CF 149), Paris, 1988, pp. 91–447 (the best study on this subject).
34. *Cf. Mystici corporis*, *AAS* 35 (1943), pp. 211–2; *Ad Sinarum gentem*, *ibid.*, 47, (1955), 9, and *Ad Apostolos principis*, *ibid.*, 50 (1958), p. 618.
35. G. Bier concludes his thesis on *Die Rechtsstellung des Diözesanbischofs nach dem Codex Iuris Canonici von 1983*, Würzburg, 2001, p. 376, thus: according to can. 480: 'The vicar general and the episcopal vicar should give an account to the diocesan bishop of the main matters to be treated and of those already treated, and they will never act contrary to the will or feeling of the diocesan bishop'.
36. *Cf.* H. Legrand, 'Le statut pluridisciplinaire de l'ecclésiologie. Une requête de LG 8', *Science et Esprit* (Ottawa) 59 (2007), pp. 333–49.
37. Increasingly direct. See art. 28 of *Ratio agendi in doctrinarum examine*, *AAS* 89 (1997), p. 834, which prohibits all appeals against a decision of the SCDF, which until now applied only to papal decisions.
38. The *Instruction* on the laity assisting the priestly ministry (1997) affirmed that 'the exclusive practice by priests of the sacrament of anointing of the sick was certain theological doctrine and secular practice', *AAS* 89 (1997), p. 39. *Cf.* note 16 supra.
40. The Archbishop of Canterbury was the first to inform Cardinal Hume of the contents of *Ad Tuendam Fidem* on the invalidity of Anglican orders. Cardinal Cassidy, President of the Pontifical Council for the Christian Unity, who had been invited to the Lambeth Conference, was told about the document only one hour before its publication. Neither of them had been consulted. Another example is the lifting of excommunication from the Lefebvrist Williamson, a Holocaust denier.
41. Paul VI noted in his Journal: 'Previously I was already isolated, but my solitude now became complete and terrible'. *Cf.* Peter Hebblethwaite, *Paul VI: the First Modern Pope*, London & Mahwah, 1993, p. 339.
42. *Cf. Annuario Pontificio*, 1954.
43. One example among others: in Austria, this led to the scandals of Bishop Kurt Krenn and especially Cardinal Hans Hermann Groer. This latter, forced to resign on account of paedophilia, was appointed without any consultation of his Abbot. Recently, the Bishops' Conference has been able to ensure that a bishop already appointed was not actually consecrated.
44. A nuncio like Mgr K. J. Rauber admits that the higher authorities rejected his suggestions more than once, *cf. Il Regno Attualità*, 65, 2010, pp. 85–86. The motives may be very diverse. For example, a cardinal of the Curia declared, well before *Summorum Pontificum*, that 'everything should be done to ensure the existence of a generation of bishops favourable to the old rite', *Trenta Giorni*, 1998, No. 11.
45. Can. 377, paragraph 3, allows the Nuncio to consult only some members of the college of advisers or the chapter, but in secret, not as a body. Indeed, consultation of the local church as such is prohibited.
46. In fact LG 22 is an argument in favour of collegiality. The relation of a bishop to his electors is not that of a Member of Parliament to his voters, because the elected bishop can only accede to his charge after his consecration by the bishops of his province, which in makes a link of communion, on the basis of the sacrament which he received.
47. Since then, only 20 Latin dioceses retain a form of right of election in Germany and in German-speaking Switzerland.
48. The text of its institution is clear: 'To allow bishops to share our concern for the universal Church, we are establishing a permanent council of bishops under our direct

and immediate authority', *AAS* 57, 1965, pp. 79–88.
49. For example, the special synod for America comprised 136 members elected by their fellow-bishops, but the majority of the synod (161) had been designated by the Pope or were ex officio members, like the cardinals of the Curia.
50. On this subject, see Hervé Legrand, 'The Roman Ministry and the Universal Ministry of the Pope. The Problems of his Election', *Concilium* 108 (1975.)
51. St Cyprian considered it an essential duty to inquire into the validity of the election of the bishop of Rome before recognizing it as such. Talk of internationalizing the college is tantamount to a secular reading of the *comprobatio*.
52. A single example: even in 2013, an 87-year-old elected cardinal was consecrated bishop. Then Cardinal Ottaviani was an ordinary priest, the Secretary of State of Pius IX was a deacon, and the last cardinal to have remained a deacon died in 1902.
53. *Address to the Participants at the Meeting of Pontifical Representatives* (21 June 2013). He hardly conceives of their ministry as that of a bishop: 'You will never teach a special section of the People of God ... you will never be at the head of a local church.'
54. According to the T. J. Reese survey, the Congregation for Bishops endorses the choice of nuncios in 80 per cent to 90 per cent of cases. See *Inside the Vatican...*, op. cit., p. 240.
55. The question has an ecumenical dimension, *cf.* Lukas Vischer 'Der Heilige Stuhl, der Vatikanstaat und das gemeinsame Zeugnis der Kirchen. Eine zu wenig diskutierte ökumenische Frage', in *Oekumenische Skizzen*, Frankfurt am Main, 1972, pp. 166–93; of course one Orthodox Church, linked to the State, was compelled to receive the Pope invited as Head of State by a government with a political interest in his visit.
56. For want of a canonical renewal comparable to the biblical, liturgical and patristic renewals, the 1983 Code is still very marked by the secularization of the thinking on canon law since 1917, as claimed by canonists themselves (cf. L. de Narois 'Canonique (droit)', *Encyclopaedia Universalis*, vol. III, pp. 880–1), but rejected by Paul VI: 'Your first preoccupation will not be to establish an judicial order modelled on civil law', 'Address to the International Congress of Canon Law of 17 September 1973', DC 70, 1973, p. 804. On these points see H. Legrand, 'Les enjeux ecclésiologiques de la codification du droit canonique', in P. Arabeyre & B. Basdevant-Gaudemet, *Les clercs et les princes. Doctrines et pratiques de l'autorité ecclésiastique à l'époque moderne (Études et rencontres de l'École des Chartes* 41), Paris, 2013, pp. 405–21. *Cf.* also note 9 supra.
57. The World Council of Churches has scarcely succeeded in showing the conciliarity of the churches. The great sacred Council of the Orthodox Church, in preparation for 50 years, is still delayed for lack of a recognized primacy.
58. *Communionis notio* 8 reminds us that: 'History shows it, when a particular Church searches to obtain its autonomy by weakening its real communion with the universal Church and its vital and visible centre, its internal unity is broken and, besides, it sees itself threatened by losing its liberty faced with multiple forces of enslavement and exploitation', *AAS* 68 (1976), pp. 54–5.

Women in the Lead: Even in the Roman Curia

SABINE DEMEL

I Introduction

There has been constant criticism of various aspects of the Roman Curia. New provisions established according to the criteria of subsidiarity, transparency and coordination are required to redress this situation. But we need more than new regulations. They will have to be accompanied by a corresponding attitude on the part of the curial staff expressed as team spirit, empathy and exemplary communication skills. Essential measures to ensure this are not only the professional rehandling of important functions and positions in the Curia but their declericalization, and the introduction of a gender-equality ordinance as well as a quota for women. If the Roman Curia were to become a pioneer and exemplar of partnership and cooperation between men and women, the resulting transformation would achieve an outstanding resonance in local churches and in society.

'We might see the Roman Curia as a venerable yet ungainly building to which features in the most varied styles have been added over the years, and possessing a façade that has been constantly repainted, without the structure ever undergoing a really thorough refurbishment.'[1] We now have a marvellously favourable opportunity to do something in this direction, since Pope Francis is evidently aiming at an exhaustive structural reform of the Roman Curia, or else he would not have established an eight-member committee to offer proposals for a planned curial reform.

But what are the criteria that could and should govern this restructuration? To date nothing in this regard has been forthcoming from the Pope himself or the committee which he appointed. Nevertheless, obvious criteria are available in terms of the constant criticisms directed against the Roman Curia.

Women in the Lead: Even in the Roman Curia

II Subsidiarity, transparency and co-ordination

The three main themes we continually come across in criticisms of the Roman Curia are its centralizing tendency, its lack of transparency and its uncoordinated character. Accordingly, the Curia needs more subsidiarity, transparency and coordination in its structure, mode of operation and forms of interaction, decision-making and etiquette. How can this transformation be achieved? Above all there is a need for practical regulations to govern the rehandling and reconstitution of existing assignments and allocations of competence, and the rights and duties of the various individual curial institutions, bodies and assemblies.

In order to reduce the degree of centralization for the sake of greater subsidiarity, a permanent bishops' council should be set up which would be referred to by and receive feedback from the Roman Curia's administration and teaching office in the exercise of its functions. As a primary result of this change it would be much more evident than in the past that the entire Church is not identical with the Roman Curia, but is the community of all local churches presided over by bishops. It would also mean that the responsibility of the bishops for and throughout the Church as a whole would have a palpable form with regard both to jurisdiction and to the magisterium. What is more, the Roman Curia would no longer intervene between Pope and bishops. The introduction of a permanent episcopal council is also advisable because 'every form of administration, including the ecclesiastical, tends to uniformity and centralization'.[2] The 'very composition of a permanent council of bishops would help to ensure greater understanding of the immense variety of solutions to problems that depend on particular cultural contexts.'[3]

Transparency would be aided by clear regulations, easily understood by and accessible to all the faithful, regarding responsibilities within the Curia, modes of procedure, and an obligation to state the reasons on which decisions are based.

To ensure coordination, it would be necessary to introduce regular and appropriately timed working discussions and seminars of the different authorities (consistories of cardinals and meetings between discasteries), for reciprocal information-gathering, advice and consultation, and mutual agreement on responsibilities and procedure. Years ago it was shown without doubt that 'the occasional meetings of dicastery directors about five times a year'[4] could not do all this. Instead, what is needed is 'a cabinet meeting regularly (weekly, to make absolutely sure) and overall collegial responsibility borne by all 'ministers' (in this case: prefects and presidents).'⁵

III Team-spirit, empathy and good communication skills

But at least as important as the introduction of these and other regulations is that a new attitude should prevail in the offices of the Roman Curia, with team spirit, empathy and communication skills as its call-signs. These key-notes will ensure that the rules are not merely documented but are actively followed. They will serve increasingly, first within the Curia itself, and then outside in the actual churches, to get rid of so much that has led to accusations of centralization, lack of transparency and absence of coordination: the frequent experience of a paradoxical state between being able to but not daring to, and between having to but not being able to; the common experience of ineffective involvement, on the one hand, and the deployment of fill-ins for a lack of staff, on the other hand; an incomprehensible tolerance of the standard ministry of absolute governance here, and the exploitation of lower ranks as the servants of the higher ranks there. The new regulations and ethos will gradually create room for reciprocal trust and confidence, for mutual recognition and participation in planning and responsibility, and for coordinated and effective cooperation for the good of the Church. But how can this attitude be implemented in the Curia, and how can we ensure that it radiates from there to the local churches?

IV Professionalization and declericalization

The important functions and positions of the Roman Curia are entirely allocated to (high-ranking) clergy. This situation is based essentially not on some kind of formal provision but on a gradual build-up of practice. In the course of time only (high-ranking) clerics were increasingly entrusted with significant duties and offices. To date, 'the rule has been that appointees to superior curial offices should have the rank of bishop. archbishop or cardinal. What would happen to high-ranking ecclesiastical dignitaries of the Curia if they could no longer fulfil their curial tasks, for whatever reasons? There are also major considerations of due legal and constiutional process. The combination of executive curial office and legislative ecclesiastical office in one and the same person grossly contradicts the principle of the separation of powers.'[6]

There are several reasons for reorganizing the division of duties and offices in the Curia, and for doing this in obedience to the principles of professionalization and declericalization. All functions that do not unconditionally call for the sacrament of ordination must no longer be allocated in accordance with the level of hierarchical orders and the dignity of rank within the ecclesiastical system.

If ordination is no longer to count as the criterion of qualification for office, but the specialist competence required for the particular function and post is to replace it, then the Curia will have to comprise many more laypeople than in the past. If a correspondingly significant weight is placed on an attitude promoting team spirit, empathy and communicative skills, then the percentage of women in the Curia will have to be very much higher. After all, gender research has shown that team spirit, empathy and communicative skills are 'soft skills', that are also generally acknowledged to be 'feminine skills' because they are capabilities that women especially are able to contribute. Insiders know that these abilities are particularly called for in the Roman Curia. Sister Judith Zoebelein, an American responsible for the web presence of the Roman Curia since its beginning in 1991, said in the course of a discussion about women in the Vatican that women have their own particular response to the circumstances and sensitivities of other people, and emphasized their communicative abilities. What better place, she remarked, could there be for the exercise of these qualities and capabilities than one whose declared goal is the diffusion of the Good News throughout the world.[7] Barbara Hallensleben, since 2003 one of two women among the 30 members of the International Theological Commission, 'the most important theological advisory body of the Holy See',[8] likes to relate how male dignitaries greeted her with statements like the following: 'It is good to have you here. The atmosphere is different now.'[9] Why is that the case? Barbara Hallensleben answers with the help of Sister Lutgart, who has worked as a translator for the Theological Commission for more than 20 years: 'She told me that she liked the new make-up of the Commission since 2003 because now there was no one there who behaved (and, interestingly enough, she used a female term) like a prima donna and tried to impose his theology on the others. I wouldn't claim that it was just the presence of the two women that had brought about this change, but it could have contributed to the new atmosphere in a small way.'[10] Sister Enrica Rosanna, undersecretary of the

Congregation for Religious Orders,[11] and thus the top-ranking woman in the Roman Curia to date, describes her special contribution as a woman in the course of her activity in the Curia with the English term 'I care'. She says that this means that 'I am concerned, I take care, you concern me, you are of interest to me, I am there for you.' Sister Enrica implements this programme in her place of work. She does so for all those who come through the door, who telephone there or send letters, but also and precisely in the circle of her co-workers. They celebrate birthdays and saints' name days and bring little Easter decorations in – and take them away too. They make sure that the atmosphere is cheerful and relaxed. They let more light in, add an eye for detail to the overall view, and recognize boundaries.[12]

V   Female quota and gender equality

But why exactly does the Roman Curia only count at most 15 per cent of women in its ranks to date,[13] and why is 'undersecretary' the highest-ranking office to which a woman has been appointed hitherto,[14] with the handful of other women acting only as secretaries and typists for the most part?[15]

Judith Zoebelein offers a simple explanation of the fact that so few women work in the Vatican. She points out that more women would have to be proposed when posts come free, but that is only possible if those in charge know qualified women personally, which, however, is a generational matter.[16] Sister Zoebelein only confirms a finding revealed by relevant studies. In 1992 a sociological study for the Rottenburg-Stuttgart diocese detected reasons for the under-representation of women at higher executive levels. One result was that the forms of recruitment and gender-specific segregation usual with regard to higher administrative levels, not only but also in the Church, were a bar to the appointment of women to executive-level positions.[17] Two structural measures are essential if we are to prevent or stop this often minimally conscious gender psychology (still) affecting the appointment of candidates to posts in the Roman Curia (too).

First, a women's quota has to be introduced urgently for leading duties and offices in the Roman Curia, and must apply until there is equality of representation for women in top posts. This quota is not an end in itself but a means to the end of eradicating the existing practice of discrimination against women. The women's quota is not a matter of preference but of stopping practices to the disadvantage and discrimination of women as far as executive posts are concerned (in the Roman Curia too).

Second, in the medium term it is necessary to introduce a formal policy of equality of opportunity and treatment for the Roman Curia involving compulsory and unequivocally formulated commitments to promote gender equality, with permanent monitoring to ensure that they are implemented. The significant innovations in this respect are regular equality analyses and monitoring of all targets, and of measures to be taken and of timetables, by a female equality-control official if at all possible. In conjunction with both the foregoing structural initiatives, it is imperative to introduce an immediate and continual process of intensive gender conscientization to inculcate appropriate self-perception, and perception of and by others, at all, and especially at the administrative, levels of the Roman Curia, together with an ongoing awareness improvement campaign to ensure not only that it is possible to identify, seriously counter and eradicate gender pitfalls, mental blocks and unconscious behaviour patterns, but that they are actually identified, countered and eradicated.

We already have a recent presentation of what these measures might entail: ' ... a woman presiding over the lay advisory council to the papacy, a woman theologian heading the Congregation for the Doctrine of the Faith, just after getting used to St Hildegard of Bingen as yet another Doctor of the Church – that would not only change the nature and operation of the Curia radically, but draw on the multitude of charisms that God has bestowed on his Church.'[18] Then there is the almost unimaginable prospect of the possible changes if ever women were appointed as papal nuncios. Think of the specifically female aspects that might come into play in the relations of the Vatican with other States and in the appointment of bishops. After all a nuntius (or nuntia) is the intermediary between the Pope and individual States and the effective source of information for the Pope on the potential candidates for a vacant episcopal see.

VI A commitment to gender-appropriate measures

For some decades now, what the Roman Curia still treats as a visionary endeavour has become an actual goal for the Evangelical Church (in Germany at least): 'Justice for women calls for their inclusion in all areas of the Church, a new division of tasks and responsibilities for men and women and gender-appropriate language[19] ... In this case, justice means that differences are acknowledged and become productive, but forms of discrimination based on those differences are out of order. A community of men and women must enable both men and women to develop and extend their abilities that have remained underdeveloped or have been repressed because of the existing division of roles and powers ... In a just community, men have to surrender their traditional privileges, depend on transformed structures, and learn new modes of behaviour in the course of dealing with women.'[20]

Not only for pragmatic reasons but on essential theological grounds, the Catholic Church cannot pretend or afford to lag behind the evident commitment of the synod of the German Evangelical Church in a resolution passed as long ago as 1989. Since Vatican II, the Catholic Church has portrayed itself as the sacrament of universal salvation, and therefore as the sign and instrument of redemption (*Lumen gentium* [The Dogmatic Constitution on the Church], 1; 9; 48: 'The Church, in Christ, is in the nature of sacrament—a sign and sacrament, that is, of communion with God and of unity among all humans' ... 'for each and every one the visible sacrament of this saving unity' ... 'The promised and hoped-for restoration ... has already begun in Christ. It is carried forward in the sending of the Holy Spirit and through him continues in the Church in which, through our faith ... we work out our salvation'). Accordingly, more than any other Church (more, indeed, than any other institution or movement), the Catholic Church has the central task of setting an example for this same world, and of ensuring that, as the Church, it becomes an unmistakable, indeed exemplary, instance of men and women living and working with equal rights and in partnership. For, ultimately, the Catholic Church draws from its faith in creation the conviction that 'the riches inherent in human beings can only emerge and reverberate as a result of the cooperative, that is, the reciprocal and complementary efforts of men and women'.[21] That this is undoubtedly the right approach is shown by the results of studies insisting that 'firms with a greater degree of heterogeneity at the decision-making level operate more innovatively and creatively. The Church can certainly make good use of innovation and creativity in the present situation.'[22]

A strong signal would surely be given to local churches as well as society in general if the imminent reform of the Roman Curia had the result not only of bringing individual women into the Curia, but of initiating a systematic process of gender equality. The message would be all the stronger if, in the course of reforming the Curia, the origins and effects of all existing values, norms and structures were scrutinized for gender-appropriateness, and they were revised to accord with the demands of gender-mainstreaming. The outcome would be even more incisive, if the 'Roman Curia' and 'gender justice' and 'equality policies' were no longer contradictory notions, and the Roman Curia were to introduce regular equality analyses and monitoring of all its targets, measures and timetable by a male or female equality-control official.

It would be truly amazing if the Roman Curia were to become the pioneer and exemplar of cooperative partnership between men and women. It would not only be a wake-up call but an immense sign of hope for the Church's capacity for reform and a powerful boost to the motivation of many disappointed and dissident women not to turn their backs on their Church.

Translated by J. G. Cumming

Notes

1. A. Zünd, 'Zur Reform der Römischen Kurie. Anregungen aus betriebswirtschaftlicher Sicht', *StZ* 218 (2000), pp. 306–14.
2. A. Gommenginger, 'Verfassung und Struktur in einem neuen Kirchenrecht', *Orientierung* 31 (1967), pp. 25–8.
3. *Ibid.*, p. 27.
4. H. Maier, 'Braucht Rom eine Regierung?', *StZ* 219 (2001), pp. 147–60, esp. p. 150.
5. *Ibid.*, p. 148.
6. A. Zünd, *op. cit.*, p. 312. According to the existing teaching of the Catholic Church on the sacred power and authority (*sacra potestas*) of popes and bishops, there can be no division of powers for pope and bishop, although that is indeed possible for the authorities of the Roman (and episcopal) Curia (*cf.* H. Heimerl, 'Menschenrechte, Christenrechte und ihr Schutz in der Kirche', *ThPQ* 121 [1973], pp. 26–35, esp. p. 32).
7. G. Sailer, 'Frauen im Vatikan. Begegnungen, Porträts, Bilder', Leipzig (n.d.), p. 79.
8. *Ibid.*, p. 122.
9. *Ibid.*, p. 125.
10. *Ibid.*, p. 125f.
11. The correct or full title of this congregation is 'the Congregation for Institutes of Consecrated Life and Societies of Apostolic Life'.
12. G. Sailer, *art. cit.*, (n. 7), p. 164.
13. *Ibid.* (n. 7). Moreover this percentage applies not only to the Roman Curia, but to the Vatican State and the Curia combined.
    Apart from this detail, no further statistics are available. The statistical yearbook issued by the Vatican contains no tabular summary to show how many people are active in the Curia. All it offers is information on population numbers per square km for every country in the world, the number of Catholics per 100 inhabitants, the number of parishes, of bishops to a country, of clerics who have left the priesthood,

of women religious, of ecclesiastical territories and so forth. The only gender-specific details provided by the yearbook concern distinctions between priests and women in religious orders. But these two groups are not directly compared (*cf.* Secretaria Status. Rationarium Generale Ecclesiae (ed.), *Annuarium statisticum Ecclesiae* 2011, Vatican City, 2013).

The following emerged from my own sampling of the 2013 edition of the papal yearbook (Segreteria di Stato, Libreria Editrice Vaticana (ed.), *Annuario Pontificio per l'anno* 2013, Vatican City, 2013): the 89 members of the Congregation for the Doctrine of the Faith include six women, one of whom works in the secretariat, four are technical assistants and one is an employee (pp. 1157–9). The 89 members of the Congregation for the Clergy include one woman, employed as a technician (p. 1189f). The Congregation for Divine Worship and the Discipline of the Sacraments comprises 100 members, none of whom is a woman (pp. 1167–9). The Pontifical Council for the Interpretation of Legislative Texts (canon law) has 74 members, including two women, both of whom as advisers (pp. 1231–2). The Apostolic Signatura comprises 44 members, including one woman assigned to the secretariat (pp. 1203–4); the Roman Rota has 52 members, again including one woman who works in the secretariat (pp. 1205–7).

14. G. Sailer, *art. cit.*, (n.7), p. 156. Information to date is that, in addition to Sister Enrica Rosanna, appointed in 2004 undersecretary of the Congregation for Religious Orders or Congregation for Institutes of Consecrated Life and Societies of Apostolic Life (see the interview 'Der Beitrag des weiblichen Genius. Interview mit der Untersekretärin der Kongregation für die Institute des geweihten Lebens' ['The woman with the top-level office on the other side of the Tiber'], accessible on http://www.30giorni.it/articoli_id_16240_l5.htm). Dr Flaminia Giovanelli has acted as undersecretary of the Pontifical Council for Justice and Peace since 2010 (see the report 'Vatikan: Zum ersten Mal wird eine Frau Untersekretärin eines Päpstlichen Rates', accessible on: http://www.zenit.org/de/articles/vatikan-zum-ersten-mal-wird-eine-frau-untersekretarin-eines-papstlichen-rates).
15. A. Zünd, *art. cit.* (n. 1), p. 312.
16. *Ibid.*,
17. A. Qualbrink, 'Fordern und Fördern. Frauen in kirchlichen Leitungspositionen', HK 65 (2011), pp. 461–6, 463, referring to C. Bender, H. Grassl, H. Motzkau & J. Schuhmacher, *Machen Frauen Kirche? Erwerbsarbeit in der organisierten Religion*, Mainz, 1996.
18. 'Papst Franziskus sollte seine Kirche grundlegend reformieren', a contribution by the guest commentator and church historian Hubert Wolf, accessible on http://www.sueddeutsche.de/panorama/reformbedarf-der-katholischen-kirche-wie-glaube-wieder-glaubwuerdig-werden-kann-1.1731252, pp. 1–5, p. 4; *cf.* also Cardinal Gottfried Daneels, Archbishop of Brussels, in an interview of 2003, accessible on http://religionv1.orf.at/projekt02/news/0309/ne030905_danneels_fr.htm.
19. A resolution of the Seventh Synod of the Evangelical Church in Germany passed at the sixth meeting on the keynote theme of the Synod: 'The Community of Men and Women in the Church', in *Bad Krozingen 1989. Bericht über die sechste Tagung der siebten Synode der Evangelischen Kirche in Deutschland vom 5. bis 10. November 1989*, Hanover, 1989, pp. 790–808, 796.
20. *Ibid.*, p. 799f.
21. D. Reininger, *Diakonat der Frau in der Einen Kirche. Diskussionen, Entscheidungen und pastoral-praktische Erfahrungen in der christlichen Ökumene und ihr Beitrag zur römisch-katholischen Diskussion*, Ostfildern, 1999, p. 650.

Women in the Lead: Even in the Roman Curia

22. A. Qualbrink, *art. cit.* (n. 7), 465; *cf.* also Daniela Engelhard, the director of the Osnabrück pastoral office: 'Experience gained in the business world shows that mixed-gender teams work more creatively and are capable of greater innovation at executive levels. It is particularly necessary to take measures to ensure that the different vocations, forms of service, and forms of existence also provide mixed-gender opportunities at executive levels in the Catholic Church' ('Die Beweislast liegt nicht bei den Frauen. Ein Gespräch mit der Osnabrücker Seelsorgeamtsleiterin Daniela Engelhard', *HK* 66 [2012], pp. 123–7).

From a Seventeenth-century Court to a Modern Service

THOMAS J. REESE, SJ

I Introduction

To convert the Roman Curia from a seventeenth-century court to a modern civil service and to incorporate the principles of collegiality and subsidiarity in church governance, it is essential to: 1. stop making curial official bishops or cardinals; 2. separate legislative, executive, and judicial functions in the Curia; 3. have curial offices supervised by committees of diocesan bishops; 4. strengthen the coordinating role of the *sostituto*; and 5. reorganize the Curia with more emphasis on regions than on functions. Reform will fail if curial officials continue to be *ex officio* bishops and cardinals.

During the general congregation meetings before the 2013 conclave, many cardinals spoke of the need to reform the Vatican. This concern was motivated by the recent Vatican scandals, both financial and sexual, as well as the general feeling that the centralization of decision-making in the Church had gone too far.

The focus of this article will be on reforming the Roman Curia, which is the part of the Vatican that assists the Pope as head of the college of bishops in governing the universal Church. It is composed of the Secretariat of State, congregations, councils, tribunals and other offices. I shall not deal with the Vatican City State, the Vatican Bank, or financial reform.[1]

During and after the Second Vatican Council (1962–5), many argued that the governance of the Church should be more collegial, and that the principle of subsidiarity should be applied to the Church so that more decisions could be made at the local level.

Some significant reforms occurred under Pope Paul VI: In 1970, cardinal electors were limited to cardinals under 80 years of age, and the

From a Seventeenth-century Court to a Modern Service

number of cardinal electors was increased to 120.[2] In 1965, the synod of bishops was created to involve the bishops in discussing issues facing the Church.[3] New curial offices (councils) were created to give attention to issues raised by Vatican II, such as ecumenism, interreligious relations, the laity, migrants, and justice and peace.[4] In 1970, 75 was set as the age of retirement for the heads of congregations and other offices, and 80 was set as the maximum age for membership on a congregation or council. More bishops from outside the Curia and outside Italy were appointed as heads of offices as well as members of congregations and councils.

The cumulative impact of these changes was to bring more and varied voices into the governance of the Church. Minor tinkering was done by John Paul II[5] and Benedict XVI, but nothing on the scale of Pope Paul. Although the Pauline reforms were significant, most people outside the Curia did not think they went far enough. As Pope Francis said to the Brazilian bishops, 'Central bureaucracy is not sufficient; there is also a need for increased collegiality and solidarity.'[6]

In spite of these reforms, the dress, style, and culture of the Vatican are still those of a papal court. The Vatican is not even a nineteenth-century bureaucracy; instead it operates like a seventeenth-century royal court where the cardinals and bishops help the Pope govern the Church just as nobles and princes helped kings govern their nations. Pope Francis is undermining this culture by his simple style and his attacks on clericalism and careerism. But structural changes are also needed if the Curia is to be converted from a court into a professional staff in service to the Pope as head of the college of bishops.

II   No ex officio cardinals or bishops

The most important reform would be is to stop making Vatican officials bishops or cardinals. A bishop or cardinal could still be appointed to the curia, but no Vatican official should ex officio be a bishop or cardinal.

Not making curial officials cardinals would eliminate their role in the election of popes. At the last conclave, about 35 percent of the electors were curial cardinals. Without any chance of participating in the election, curial officials could focus on their work rather than on politicking for the next conclave. This reform would emphasize the Pope's connection to bishops around the world and provide around 40 additional red hats for distribution to diocesan bishops.

Not making curial officials bishops or cardinals would make clear that they are not part of the magisterium or a governing elite, but staff to the Pope as head of the college of bishops. There is no necessary connection between being a curial official and being a member of the college of bishops. Before John XXIII, many curial officials were not bishops even if they were cardinals. Such a reform would make clear that the Curia is in service to the college of bishops, not superior to it. Curial officials, including nuncios, who are not cardinals or archbishops, would be more respectful in their dealings with diocesan bishops.

Not making curial officials bishops or cardinals would also give the Pope more flexibility in appointing and removing them. The Pope could bring in a priest to direct an office for temporary period and then return him to his diocese or religious order. And if an appointment does not work out, it is easier to send a priest back to his diocese than to get rid of an archbishop or cardinal. It would also open up the possibility of appointing laymen and women to many of these jobs.

An important consequence of not making curial officials cardinals or bishops would be that they could not be members of an ecumenical council or the synod of bishops. This would allow for more diocesan bishops in the synod and strengthen the synod's connection to local churches. Curial officials could attend synods and ecumenical councils as staff to listen and answer questions, but not to vote.

Finally, not making curial officials bishops or cardinals would provide a severe blow to careerism in the Vatican. Priests could no longer look at working in the Vatican as a way of moving up the ecclesiastical ladder. If a priest wanted to be a bishop or cardinal, he would have to leave the Curia. This reform is essential to converting the Curia from a seventeenth-century court into something like a modern civil service.

III Separation of powers

In the time of absolute monarchs, the king had supreme legislative, executive, and judicial power. Contemporary political theory sees the need for separating these powers in order to avoid the abuse of power. Even if the Pope holds such power, it would be better for the Curia to be organized with a separation of power.

Today, many congregations determine policies or laws (legislative power), enforce these policies and laws (executive), and pass judgment on those who violate them (judicial). This can be seen, for example, in the treatment of theologians by the Congregation for the Doctrine of the Faith (CDF), which acts as lawgiver, police investigator, prosecutor, judge, and jury. In civil society, this would be considered a violation of due process.

How could the Curia be organized to give greater weight to the principle of the separation of powers?

Currently, the Curia is organized with committees called congregations and councils that oversee the work of an office. The head of the office (prefect for congregations and president for councils) is also chairman of the committee. Many members of the committees are heads of other offices in the Curia. In a reformed Curia, the only members of the committees would be diocesan bishops from outside the Curia, one of whom would be chair. Increasing the role of diocesan bishops would better reflect the collegiality of the Church.

These members might be chosen or nominated by the synod of bishops or by bishops' conferences. Under such a system, the members would be chosen to represent the views of the bishops rather than simply be bishops who have friends in the papal court. For example, the Congregation for Divine Worship might have on it chairs of episcopal conference liturgy committees. Major policy decisions or changes in law would have to be reviewed by these committees.

In the past, it was difficult for diocesan bishops to come to Rome for meetings. Today, technology makes it possible to attend meetings without travelling to Rome.

A separate department of justice should be created to investigate and prosecute criminal behaviour in the Church, including crimes like sexual abuse, financial corruption, dereliction of duty, and abuse of power. Following the principle of subsidiarity, such a department of justice would only deal with cases that could not be dealt with on the local or regional level, or that come to Rome on appeal. For example, such an office could investigate a bishop accused of covering up sexual abuse crimes by his priests.

Judicial functions should be separated from the prosecutorial. Having these functions performed by different persons in the same office is not an adequate separation of powers. Perhaps retired bishops could act as judges and/or juries in cases brought by curial prosecutors against bishops.[7]

Thomas J. Reese SJ
IV Coordination in the Vatican

One of the arguments in favour of keeping curial officials as members of Vatican congregations and councils is that it helps in coordinating policy. In reality, this could be better done by ad hoc task-forces or committees dealing with specific issues or problems that overlap the jurisdiction of offices. In addition, in modern governments such coordination is done through the office of the president or prime minister. In the Vatican, the first or 'ordinary' section of the Secretariat of State has played a similar rôle. The second or 'extraordinary' section is the foreign ministry of the Vatican.[8]

The *sostituto* (substitute) heads the first section and reports directly to the Pope and the secretary of state. The equivalent position in government would be that of the chief of staff to a president or prime minister. Under Paul VI, Archbishop Giovanni Benelli wielded great power from this position, but his successors did not.

The weakness of the *sostituto* led to others performing the coordinating function. For example, any document touching on church teaching has to be reviewed by the Congregation for the Doctrine of the Faith before it can be issued. Disagreements between offices over draft documents are more likely to be settled by the CDF than by the *sostituto*. This system of coordination worked under John Paul II because he had great confidence in Cardinal Ratzinger, who made sure that no document was released by the Curia unless it was in harmony with his and John Paul's views. Under Francis, on the other hand, CDF's supremacy was challenged when Cardinal Joao Braz de Aviz of the Congregation for Religious publicly complained about not being consulted on CDF's investigation of the Leadership Council of Women Religious.

The influence of the papal secretary, Mgr Stanislaw Dziwisz, also grew over time during the papacy of John Paul. Dziwisz often determined which people and documents were seen by the Pope. Dziwisz knew the mind of the Pope and had the his ear and confidence. When queries were addressed to the Pope, the secretary responded as the Pope's voice even when the Pope was not consulted. In earlier papacies, these functions were performed by the *sostituto*, but during the papacy of John Paul, even *sostitutos* deferred to Dziwisz.

Within the Vatican, the secretary of state is second only to the Pope. Despite having the same name as the US secretary of state, he is more like a prime minister than a foreign minister. Besides supporting the

From a Seventeenth-century Court to a Modern Service

Pope's agenda and priorities, he must handle matters in which the Pope has little interest. For example, John Paul had a deep understanding of and interest in Eastern Europe, but less in Latin America. With Francis, the opposite will be the case.

Just as a prime minister must concern himself with both domestic and foreign policy, so too the secretary of state must deal with internal church issues and foreign policy; that is why there are two sections in the secretariat of state. Neither the Pope nor the secretary of state have the time to micromanage the Curia, but someone has to mind the store. The logical person is the *sostituto*.

A smoothly-running Curia requires a powerful *sostituto* who has the complete confidence of the Pope. The *sostituto* needs a competent staff of canon lawyers, theologians, and other experts to make sure that the Pope's agenda and priorities are reflected in the work of the Curia. Inevitably he will make enemies because he is the one who has to say No to people, or force them to do things they don't want to do. Without the backing of the Pope, curial officials can ignore him and run circles round him.

V Reorganizing the offices in the Curia

The current organization of the Curia has more to do with history than any organizational plan.[9] For example, to understand the work of the Congregation for the Clergy one has to remember that it was originally founded in 1564 as the Congregation of the Council, whose job was to oversee the implementation of the reforms of the Council of Trent. The major topics of reform coming out of the council—seminaries, clergy, catechetics, local church finances—became and remained the agenda of the congregation despite five centuries and two subsequent councils.

Likewise, relations with Jews are handled by the Council for the Promotion of Christian Unity, not the Council for Interreligious Dialogue, because Jewish groups already had a relationship with the office of Christian unity going back to the Second Vatican Council, and they did not want to switch. Good relations trumped organizational purity.

The Curia is further complicated by the fact that responsibilities in the Curia are divided among the dicasteries in different ways. Some responsibilities are divided by the type of church (Oriental, Latin missionary, Latin non-missionary); some by issues (ecumenism, doctrine, liturgy, or social communications); and some by the people affected (bishops, clergy, religious, laity, health-care workers).

Any large multinational organization faces similar problems in organizing. To what extent should an organization's structure be based on geographical regions, product lines, or functions (finances, personnel, sales and so on)? Getting different parts of the organization to work together smoothly is a challenge in any organization. Empowering regional offices improves responses to customers, whereas stressing product or functional offices supports uniformity. When a multinational corporation gets the mix wrong, market share and profits fall.

Because of the way the Curia is organized, bishops and religious superiors report being interrogated about the same issue by a multitude of curial offices. Sometimes the involvement of all these offices can be confusing to outsiders. For example, Cardinal Lopez Trujillo as the head of the Council on the Family condemned the sex education in a book that had an imprimatur by Archbishop Daniel Pilarczyk. To the uninitiated it looked as if the archbishop was defying the Vatican when in fact the cardinal had no authority to do what he did.

Before trying to reorganize the Curia, it is important to acknowledge there is no perfect organizational structure that will ensure everything runs smoothly. Each approach has its strengths and weaknesses. Nor would a bureaucracy with no conflicts or disagreements serve the needs of the Pope. If everyone in the Curia agreed on everything there would be no room for creativity and debate. Disagreements bring important issues to the attention of the Pope. A major problem with the papacies of John Paul and Benedict was that there was little room for disagreements and debate on issues facing the Church. On the other hand, disagreements become dysfunctional when they result from personality conflicts and bureaucratic turf wars.

As I mentioned earlier, some congregations deal with different types of churches: the Congregation for Oriental Churches, the Congregation for Evangelization of Peoples (missionary churches), and the Congregation for Bishops (Latin, non-missionary churches). Because of their unique history, spirituality, liturgy, laws, and practices, the oriental churches require special treatment. But how much longer should the Vatican treat 'missionary' churches separately from the older churches? Today the Church is more alive in parts of Africa than it is in parts of Europe, yet Africa is still treated as missionary territory.

The Congregation for Evangelization of Peoples is an anachronism and should be phased out. Perhaps both it and the Congregation for Bishops could be replaced by five offices dealing with different regions of the Church: Europe, Africa, Latin America, North America and Asia. Each could have a supervisory committee of diocesan bishops primarily from its region. Such offices would provide 'for a greater appreciation of local and regional elements', as desired by Pope Francis. What is needed is 'not unanimity, but true unity in the richness of diversity'.[10]

The rôle of these offices would be subject to the principle of subsidiarity, which would call for greater involvement of local churches and conferences of bishops, including in the appointment of bishops. These offices could also deal on a regional basis with questions that previously were dealt with by the Congregation for Clergy and the Council on the Laity, and could report to the department of justice any cases that need investigation and prosecution.

There would still be a need for offices dealing with important topics like liturgy and church teaching. Since the Congregation for the Doctrine of the Faith would no longer prosecute or judge theologians or deal with abusive priests, its rôle could become more creative. It could become the Congregation for the Development of Church Teaching. Its mandate would be to encourage theologians to come up with new ways of explaining the Christian faith to people of the twenty-first century. This would involve both sophisticated work in the area of science and religion, and creative approaches to evangelization and religious education. In other words, it would become the research and development office of the Church rather than the Inquisition. Such a congregation could also replace the Congregation for Education and the Council for the New Evangelization.

Issues of special concern to the Pope and the Church (ecumenism, justice and peace, interreligious dialogue and son) could still have separate offices to make sure that their issues are not lost in the bureaucracy, but they might include sunset provisions so that future popes can extend their lives or let them die as priorities change. For example, global warming may be the most critical issue of this century and therefore might deserve a separate office.

VI Conclusion

I repeat: the most important reform, without which all other reforms will be meaningless, is to stop making curial officials cardinals and bishops.

Thomas J. Reese SJ

As long as curial officials are made cardinals and archbishops, they will act as if they are superior to the college of bishops instead of staff to the Pope as head of the college of bishops. Such a reform will also strengthen the Pope's ability to appoint and remove officials in the Curia without worrying about giving them another assignment of equal or greater status. Without such a reform, the Curia may suffer a setback to its power under Pope Francis, but it will regain its position under subsequent popes.

Changes in procedures are just as important as organizational changes. For example, issuing more draft documents and regulations for public discussion and comment would lead to better results.

Reforming the Vatican will not bring about the Kingdom of God, but, if properly done, it can provide the organizational structure that better serves the Pope, the college of bishops, and the People of God, who through prayer and works of charity and justice do make the reign of God present in the world. No organizational structure is perfect, which is why it must be continuously examined and reformed as the Church and popes learn through experience and adapt to new circumstances.

Notes
1. For an examination of Vatican finances, see Thomas J. Reese, SJ, *Inside the Vatican: The Politics and Organization of the Catholic Church*, Cambridge, MA, 1996, Chapter 8.
2. For the history and role of the College of Cardinals, see *ibid.*, Chapter 4.
3. On the synod of bishops, see *ibid.*, Chapter 3.
4. Paul VI, *Regimini Ecclesiae universae* (1967).
5. John Paul II, *Pastor Bonus* (1988). For an analysis of the constitution, see Piero Antonio Bonnet & Carlo Gullo (eds), *La Curia Romana nella Cost. Ap. 'Pastor Bonus'*, Studi Giuridici, vol. 21, Vatican City, 1990; James H. Provost, 'Pastor Bonus: Reflections on the Reorganization of the Roman Curia', *Jurist*, 48 (1988), pp. 499–535; Joël-Benoît d'Onorio, *Le Pape et le Gouvernement de L'Église*, Paris, 1992.
6 Pope Francis, Address at the Meeting of the Bishops of Brazil, 28 July 2013.
7. An extensive discussion of Vatican tribunals is beyond the scope of this article. The Roman Rota deals primarily with marriage annulments, and if the annulment process is simplified, the work of the Rota could be eliminated or reduced. Likewise, the work of the Signatura as a court of appeals would be reduced if more cases were dealt with locally according to the principle of subsidiarity. On the other hand, its work might be expanded beyond dealing simply with procedural questions. For more on tribunals, see chapter 5, *Inside the Vatican*.
8. For a description of the role of the first and section sections of the secretariat of state, see chapter 7, *Inside the Vatican*.
9. For more on the organization of the Vatican congregations and councils, see Inside the Vatican, *op. cit.*, chapter 5.
10. Pope Francis, Address at the Meeting of the Bishops of Brazil, 28 July 2013.

Renewal and Clarity in the Government of the Church

CELSO QUEIROZ OSB

I Introduction

This article is based on my pastoral experience as a bishop with responsibilities in the bishops' conference of my country. My intention is to describe and discuss the reintroduction of the collegial government of the Church by the Second Vatican Council, the problem of centralization and the resulting expansion of the Roman Curia, with special reference to the diplomatic corps and the apostolic nunciatures. I also refer to situations of misunderstanding and embarrassment caused by ignorance, careerism and so on, and ask why these posts should not be open to lay-people.

II A complex mixture

I worked in the Secretariat of the Brazilian bishops' conference before and after becoming a bishop with a long period of ministry after Vatican II. This prompted *Concilium* to ask me to write about the need for and the possibility of renewal in the apostolic nunciatures as a specific aspect of the relation between papal government and the bishops' conferences. Of course I discuss this subject as a bishop and not as a technical expert on a diplomatic corps or mechanism, or on the basis of information and historical analysis regarding the formation of this diplomatic corps of the Church.

The Church's diplomatic apparatus was established in the political context of complex and often conflictive relations between 'throne and altar' in the era of sacred monarchies and power disputes. Admittedly, there have been significant developments since then. From the nineteenth century onwards these changes produced an increasingly complex mixture, that is, a form of hybridization, of strictly ecclesial relations between the papal government and the local churches, and political aspects of the Catholic Church such as the Vatican State and the modern States with which the Vatican maintains diplomatic relations. The apostolic nunciatures are in the middle here. They present credentials and take part in state ceremonies, even in the case of corrupt and bloody dictatorships, and may even work on complex concordats, but they are also channels of the Church's internal government. They are a means of making episcopal appointments, and involve inevitable internal politics and what are in practice exorbitant powers. It is legitimate to ask whether they create an anomalous situation in relations between episcopates and the papal government or, more radically, in ecclesiology itself.

Theoretically, apostolic nunciatures are a service and provide a link between the papal government and other instances. From a bishop's pastoral viewpoint, however, policies dictated by individuals or interest groups lead not only to considerable ambiguity in this diplomatic machine but, inevitably, to undesirable collateral effects. The people of God constantly and insistently call for renewal, participation and transparency instead of excessive secrecy about the criteria and procedures for the choice and appointment of bishops. This demand can no longer be ignored.

III The episcopate as the governing power in the Church

The First Vatican Council was the end-point of a long process of centralization in the Church. This was not a necessary outcome of the dogma of papal infallibility, but a narrow interpretation of infallibility did set the seal on that centralization. It now seemed only logical to dispense with councils, and the ministry of bishops was gradually understood and treated as one of acting as local curates for the Pope. The purity of faith and the communion of all Christendom were guaranteed in and through the Pope. Many bishops understood their episcopal ministry in this way. In order to undertake its broad jurisdictional mission (even though, given its accumulation of 'universal, immediate and ordinary' powers, any such mission was practically impossible[1]), the papacy surrounded itself with a considerable number of assistants in Rome (the Roman Curia) and around the world (the apostolic nunciatures, coordinated by the Secretariat of State). These assistant 'commanders' relied on a sacramental, sacral, concept of hierarchy that gave them a position in the sacral order that was higher than, or at least equal to, that of their 'subordinates'. Of course this arrangement was and remains reminiscent of a pre-modern feudal system. Cardinals, archbishops and monsignors compose a sacred hierarchy, and are involved in a web of ecclesiastical honours. But, from a modern viewpoint, we can also envisage lay-people operating an equivalent system with a merely functional hierarchy. Historians of religion, perhaps even religious anthropologists, can account for the existing accumulation of hierarchical sacrality. But it has nothing to do with the Gospel of Jesus.

The strictly practical result of this sacral system was that the Pope no longer needed the episcopal college as a partner to run the Church throughout the world. After all, it was not without opposition, and only after long debate, that Vatican II defined the Church as 'governed by the successor of Peter and the bishops in communion with him' (LG 8), and stated that in their ministry bishops, 'in virtue of the unbroken succession, going back to the beginning, are regarded as transmitters of the apostolic line' (LG 20). Therefore 'this power, which they exercise personally in the name of Christ, is proper, ordinary and immediate, although its exercise is ultimately controlled by the supreme authority of the Church ... nor are they to be regarded as vicars of the Roman Pontiff; for they exercise the power which they possess in their own right' (LG 27). Bishops' authority is not 'damaged', but 'defended, upheld and strengthened' by 'the supreme and universal power' (LG 27).

The Council also noted the respect due to groups of churches with their own discipline, liturgy and theological and spiritual traditions. Moreover, 'in a like fashion the episcopal conferences at the present time are in a position to contribute in many and fruitful ways to the concrete realization of the collegiate spirit' (LG 23).

IV Excessive centralization

As Vatican II drew to a close, a consensus emerged among the participants. This held that the appropriate instrument to enable the action of the episcopal college headed by the Pope to take effect would be a permanent synod-like body of bishops. Yet this idea was reduced to a regular meeting, mainly for study, with a merely consultative role in support of the Pope. This does not represent the Council's intention.[2]

The Roman Curia is the body that really functions in the central government of the Church throughout the world. But the Roman Curia, with its current size and power, is the result of a concept of the Church, and of an ecclesiology, exclusively centred on the person of the Pope as the guarantee of its unity. At some moments in history, in the distant past, this kind of compact centralization of jurisdiction might well have benefited the unity of the Church. Yet, at the very beginning of the greatest process of centralization, at the start of the second millennium, one result of centralization was a traumatic and painful break between West and East. But any such centralization has become dysfunctional. The Church's centralized government is necessarily confined and conditioned by a vast bureaucracy that lays it open to the risks characteristic of all bureaucracy, such as power struggles, careerism, corruption, concealment of information, delay and the blocking of new ideas. There is an added, fatal, risk in the Church: that of confusion between bureaucracy and priestly hierarchy, which has the effect of sacralizing the bureaucracy itself, and thus making it (like everything sacred) almost 'untouchable'.

V Decentralization and the college

Centralization, therefore, lies behind the inflation of the Roman Curia. Centralization was adopted to ensure the unity of the Church in various cultures and regions of the world. The degree of centralization was even greater in the past than it is now. Vatican II introduced some efforts to reduce it, but we need to go further, and move from the centre to the various outlying areas. We need a genuine confluence of these regions towards the centre in a real catholicity. Furthermore, we cannot allow the quest for new pastoral expressions and methods to be prohibited with the simultaneous promotion of a reversion to old rites in a dead language, and to formulas alien to today's cultures. The unity of the Church does not reside in languages or cultures from the past which deserve the respectful acknowledgement of a place of honour in our museums. The Church's unity lies much deeper, in the unity of faith and essentials that flow from a common faith. If the unity needed to cultivate what is essential is guaranteed, the rest can be left to the bishops of each country or region, without any need for approval from an authority other than the bishops.

The Vatican II made possible a degree of contact between the episcopates of various nations that had never existed between bishops in the modern world. Bishops learned from the Council that they were not merely heads of local or particular churches, but co-responsible for the universal Church.

As Archbishop Helder Câmara showed so forcefully, they are 'catholic' bishops. After Vatican II, it became usual for bishops from what was then called the 'Third World' to be invited to talk to the churches of more developed nations about problems confronting poor countries. They were listened to attentively. Helder Câmara himself was also a great example in this process. But before long these bishops were summoned to Rome and warned that they were acting beyond the bounds of their dioceses, and should stop trying to exercise a mission reserved to the Pope. Something similar occurred with a project of the Brazilian bishops' conference to study cases of oppression in under-developed countries. I was involved in this as a conference official. In contradiction of what the Council says about the collegial mission of bishops, together with the Pope, in world evangelization, Rome ordered each bishop and each conference to limit themselves to their own country and to their own diocese.[3]

In the face of new pastoral issues, which forced them to produce new ideas on structures, bishops with a considerable reputation as pastors found the doors of the relevant curial departments closed. This happened to us in the archdiocese of São Paulo. A long investigation of ways of dealing with the challenge to the Church posed by our huge megalopolis gave rise to a proposal to give each region of the huge urban area the presence and ministry of a bishop, a council of priests, a pastoral council and other bodies, without dividing the city into totally autonomous dioceses. This move was intended to avoid both the danger of a fragmented response to the organic logic of the city, and the traditional practice of appointing a number of auxiliary bishops. It was a new proposal for interdependent dioceses, and abandoned the concept of the diocese as a territory around a bishop monarch in favour of the conciliar notion of the diocese as part of the people of God governed collegially. The proposal was not discussed. It was not even granted the courtesy of an acknowledgment. The city was simply divided into dioceses as if they were adjacent territories. For example, the Marian shrine of Our Lady, patroness of the city, at the centre of the archdiocese was left in an outlying diocese, outside the reduced archdiocesan territory, and the residence of São Paulo's state governor was also relegated to an outlying diocese.

VI Apostolic nunciatures in the middle

In reality, real direct access to the Pope for bishops and their conferences continues to be very difficult and sometimes impossible. The Curia and especially the apostolic nunciatures come between Pope and bishops. In certain circumstances, nunciatures, as the diplomatic representatives of the Vatican to the governments of every country with which the Vatican maintains diplomatic relations, can make the Church's mission easier.[4] As Pietro Parolin, the new Vatican Secretary of State, said before taking up his post, the role of the Church's diplomatic mission is the promotion of peace and human rights in the world.

In other circumstances, however, history shows that concordats can be ambivalent. Some can make things easy for both sides, while others do the opposite, give privileges, produce constraints and create resentment. A specific current example is the 2008 agreement signed between the Vatican and the Brazilian government. On the one hand, it made no difference to the situation that had obtained for more than a century, since the proclamation of the secular Republic. From that time the State has had no obligation to grant any favour to the Church and the Church has had no obligations towards the State. On the other hand, the new agreement is under examination by the Brazilian courts since it is suspected of unconstitutionality in certain points that grant privileges and create an anomaly in the State's secular character. It has also created bad feeling in ecumenical relations. Furthermore, the bishops' conference, which was neither consulted adequately nor discussed the text sufficiently to give it final approval, now finds itself obliged to defend what may turn out to be indefensible. If what is provided for in this agreement is valid for any Church that wants the same status, why do we need a specific agreement? A nuncio's triumph has become a pastoral burden for the bishops.

When a nuncio, in his representative role, is seen by the media at political parties and dinners alongside government figures of dubious morals, this only increases the embarrassment of the bishops of local churches. In practice, however, the nunciature takes little interest in representing the Vatican State and the Pope as its sovereign. Its real business is church affairs, and in this role it acquires great power over local churches. Examples of this development are the appointments, transfers and 'promotions' of bishops and all the information sent to Rome without the local bishops, even the conference through its presidency, having access to the processes. If mistakes occur through lack of wider dialogue, the price is paid by the local church and its bishops.

The role of the nunciatures is possibly less decisive in countries where

Renewal and Clarity in the Government of the Church

the Christian tradition is more ancient and church structures are more solid. But it is very important in younger countries, such as those of Latin America, and even more so in Africa and Asia. The difference in treatment follows from the variable attitude towards the different parts of the world and their churches. This explains the minimal fuss when a nuncio in our region calmly remarked to the bishops: '"Continent" means Europe. The rest of the world is just islands, big ... but simply islands.' This remark, which might be taken as a joke, in fact hides a serious problem in the diplomatic and, above all, internal relations of the Church, which is the level of knowledge or ignorance about the countries and the local churches in which they function shown by diplomatic representatives. A current example of bad diplomacy, which created a deep wound and almost a national riot in Latin America, concerns the diocese of Sucumbíos in Ecuador. It is difficult to know what kind of ecclesiological or political principles led to the disastrous situation in which the Carmelite bishop was removed, only to be replaced by 'Heralds of the Gospel', who came into the diocese in their heavy boots and trampled over its people, who may have been uneducated but knew that they were the people of God.[5]

Certain facts will help these comments not to become too abstract or idealistic. One embarrassing practice which infantilizes bishops and local churches is that in regions like Latin America, where most churches are younger than elsewhere, the bishops avoid adopting any attitude of disagreement with the nunciature for fear of being disobedient to the Pope. The cause may be timidity, fear of 'being marked', or even perhaps concern to 'preserve your career', which was the unashamed advice of one secretary at the nunciature in Brazil. As a result, bishops often invite the nuncio, as 'the Pope's representative', to preside at the most important ceremonies in the diocese, precisely at times when a reputable ecclesiology would require the diocesan bishop to lead his local church.

VII Nuncios' attitudes

In my long experience of work in executive bodies of the bishops' conference, I have witnessed a nuncio acting towards the assembled bishops as though he was the national authority on liturgy or liturgical vestments. Then I observed one (and this is really serious) attempt to ban a bishop from talking at a course for fellow bishops on the battle against hunger. On another occasion, a nuncio tried to stop a bishop accepting an invitation to speak at a national priests' meeting. On these and other occasions nuncios were intent on prohibiting the efforts of those with prophetic attitudes, or in favour of a Church in touch with the real world, or opposing injustice and concerned with the poor. I end my account with the most arbitrary behaviour I have witnessed. The retired Bishop Clemente Isnard, a genial sage (now dead) who did great things to promote the reforms of Vatican II, wrote a booklet about aspects of church structure which he felt needed rethinking, questions which we are all concerned with today. He had been vice-president of the Brazilian bishops' conference, vice-president of the Latin American Episcopal Council (CELAM), responsible for the application of Vatican II's liturgical reform, and a constant figure of reference in this field. The Brazilian bishops' conference had sent him as a delegate on a particularly delicate mission to the Holy Father. The nuncio heard about the booklet, telephoned all the national Brazilian Catholic publishers, and forbade its publication, on the ground that it might damage the Church. Bishop Isnard's text appeared only when a small secular publisher accepted it. It generated a very good discussion, with no damage to the Church. But this provokes further questions. Is this an exception among the churches of Latin America, Africa and Asia? What motives lie behind this infantilizing behaviour by a nunciature? Is it fear of damaging the nuncio's career? Isn't this the product of a bureaucracy that is losing its way and becoming corrupted by the web of interests which I referred to earlier?

VIII Conclusion

Clearly, conceiving the very existence of nunciatures as intelligible only in terms of the Church as a sovereign State governed by a monarch does not accord with the Vatican II notion of the State. But how are we to incorporate apostolic nunciatures in the collegial government of the bishops together with the Pope without creating anomalies in conciliar ecclesiology? Admittedly, a diplomatic service allows the Church a presence among the family of nations and in international organizations where it can campaign for gospel values, such as the dignity of the human person and life, freedom, peace, the fight against starvation, aid to poorer nations, and so on. Nunciatures can certainly help bishops' conferences, bishops and local churches when they have problems, but they cannot place themselves above the bishops, local churches and the bishops' conferences of the countries where they are stationed. That would mean promoting a collision between the prophetic dimension of the Church and the diplomatic logic of its historical existence, as has happened even in modern times, to the detriment of the prophetic dimension.

Obviously reforming the system of church government and the bodies responsible for it is neither simple or easy. We have made little progress in this area in the 50 years since Vatican II. Part of the problem is that one aspect cannot be changed without affecting the others. As a result, in order to make the mission of the episcopal college with regard to the Church present in the world we need to scale down the Roman Curia and focus diplomacy more effectively. We also need to give the Pope a body of bishops that can exercise genuine co-responsibility and be more than a synod that meets for study sessions every few years. It is equally important to allow bishops' conferences to decide everything that is not part of our unity in faith, and that ought to represent the richness of communion lived out in the diversity of the churches.

Finally, in all these aspects it is possible to open up spaces for a real participation of lay-people, to abandon the narrow world of clericalism, and to enrich decisions with the diverse experiences of various vocations. Why should a bishop, whose episcopal consecration is directed to the service of a diocese, hold the post of ambassador or head of a Vatican department? Surely the department for religious can be headed by a nun with experience in the government of her congregation, since, after all, three-quarters of religious are women. Surely the presidency of Pontifical Councils can be held by individuals who do not belong to the priestly hierarchy. Surely we can follow a model that has proved its efficacy in modern society and see that the role of nuncio can be exercised more appropriately by lay men or women, since they are baptized Catholics who are capable of representing the Church in the spheres of politics and administration, and various documents of the magisterium insist that politics is the sphere of lay-people (both men and women). What prevents the pontifical diplomatic academy from training Catholic lay-people for this role?

Translated by Francis McDonagh

Notes

1. 'If the (Roman) Catholic Church were to define her mission in terms of synergy and at a juridical level to develop *subsidiarity* in her relations with other sees, would this obscure her deep conviction about the Roman "primate"? If one admits, as every (Roman) Catholic loyal to his Church does, that God has willed the office of the bishop of Rome, how can we think that God wants what it has gradually turned into? How, in his wisdom and intelligence, could he have wished to load on to the shoulders of the "primate" a task so heavy and complex that no normally healthy man could carry it out without ruining his health and power to work, or surrounding himself with a bureaucracy so heavy that it acts as a break on his wishes and his insights as the one responsible for sustaining the *koinonia*? In a very intelligent contribution to the discussions of Vatican I, Mgr Ketteler, bishop of Mainz, a member of the Minority, said that to confer on the pope an ordinary and immediate jurisdiction over all the faithful was to give him a task that it was impossible in practice to carry out. This is even more true in our century, which has seen the flourishing of missionary movements which have meant the introduction into catholicity of new cultures and new human situations' (J. M. R. Tillard, *The Bishop of Rome*, London, 1983, pp. 189–90).
2. As Hervé Legrand showed in 'Forty Years Later: What has become of the Ecclesiological Reforms envisaged by Vatican II?' (*Concilium* 2005/4, pp. 57–72), one of the factors that led to the Council being 'cheated' was the difference between its documents and the 1983 Code of Canon Law. The Council did not produce binding guidelines except in the document on the liturgy and in some points of the document on bishops. The other documents are theological and pastoral, but were not properly translated into rules subsequently. The result was a kind of schizophrenia between the Church as the people of God governed collegially and the monarchical pyramid structure, which remained untouched.
3. It is curious that another type of relationship, consisting of missionary visits from bishops from developed countries to their brothers in impoverished dioceses, did not create the same level of upset.
4. The Vatican, as 'the Church's State', obviously has an historical explanation that sells many books. In the eyes of other Churches, it is something unique and would appear bizarre unless its existence was understood in terms of history rather than the Gospel. In some countries the fact that the Reformed Churches or the Anglican Church are established has no more than formal consequences. The Vatican, however, retains its vitality, maintains its position in the United Nations, and its whole enormous and costly diplomatic corps. The value of this system has been assessed from a great variety of viewpoints, but my concern here is the internal relationships within the government of the Church itself.
5. *Cf Concilium* 2011/5.

Part Three: Spiritual, Pastoral and Ecumenical Dimensions

Ecumenical Implications of Reforming the Curia

WALTER ALTMANN

I Introduction

In this article I raise the question of how far the reform of the Curia, in principle a matter of the internal economy of the Catholic Church, is relevant to ecumenical relations. I note advances achieved in dialogue as well as the loss of the original enthusiasm for the cause of ecumenism. Nevertheless, since the differences between the Churches are today largely focused on ecclesiological issues, I conclude that precisely the reform of the Curia has the potential to contribute to a greater coming together, understanding and cooperation between the different Christian denominations.

Should a Lutheran pastor and theologian who holds a prominent position in the World Council of Churches (WCC) express an opinion on the reform of the Roman Curia in the Catholic Church? After all, this is above all a question of the Catholic Church's internal organization, and the proper attitude of an ecumenical partner must be always one of complete respect, whatever the decisions to be taken. I pondered this question when I received an invitation to write in the prestigious journal *Concilium*.

In the end I accepted the invitation and the challenge from the editors, although I hadn't reached a definitive answer to my own question. I agreed, however, because whatever decisions are taken on the reform of the Roman Curia, they will inevitably have repercussions on the relationships between Christian denominations. And one of the urgent tasks in these relationships, though always a thorny one, is that of strengthening efforts to achieve the unity of the Christian family.

II Recovering our courage for the ecumenical journey

It is no secret that ecumenism today does not arouse the enthusiasm of the early days, whether that of the World Missionary Conference in Edinburgh in 1910, or that which surrounded the creation of the WCC in Amsterdam in 1948, or again when a large group of Orthodox churches joined the WCC at its Third Assembly in New Delhi (1961), or that provoked by the clear commitment to ecumenism by the Second Vatican Council (1962–5). With regard to the Council, it should be noted that the spirit of ecumenism permeated the whole of Vatican II, and is not confined to its Decree on Ecumenism (*Unitatis redintegratio*), but is present in other conciliar documents, such as the Dogmatic Constitution on Divine Revelation (*Dei verbum*).

It is not like that today, we have to admit. We are often told that ecumenism has lost its impetus and that the Churches have channelled their efforts inwards in an attempt to strengthen their own denominational identity and institutional organization, and have neglected their involvement with and commitment to ecumenism.

My view is that this judgment is only partly true, because there can be no doubt of the many advances ecumenism has achieved during recent decades. Today the atmosphere between the great historical denominations is marked by a mutual respect unthinkable in earlier centuries. There are also countless examples of cooperation between the Churches, not only at local and regional level, but also at a global institutional level. Many bilateral theological dialogues have brought notable advances in doctrinal understanding. In Catholic–Lutheran dialogue, for example, we can cite the solemn signing in Augsburg in 1999 of the *Joint Declaration on the Doctrine of Justification*, the core issue in dispute in the Reformation period, the article described by Luther as that by which the Church stands or falls (*articulus stantis et cadentis Ecclesiae*). Another example is the recent report of the Lutheran–Roman Catholic International Commission on Unity, with the significant title *From Conflict to Communion*, which proposes a common Lutheran–Catholic commemoration of the Reformation in 2017. The report attempts for the first time to set out a common vision of the sixteenth-century Reformation, though one that includes differences, gives an overview of the results of the official Lutheran–Catholic dialogue in the 50 years leading up to the 2017 anniversary, and presents the theological agenda for the future in the bilateral dialogue.

Some weighty theological differences persist, many of them in the sphere of ecclesiology and Church organization. They have so far made it impossible not only to ensure that the longed-for unity becomes reality, but apparently even push it to a far horizon. Many church members cannot understand the difficulty the Churches have in translating the theological advances into practice, especially our separation at the Lord's Table. Pastoral sensitivity therefore requires that in our ecumenical enterprise the dominant attitude should not be discouragement, but perseverance and (why not?) something of that boldness to which the apostles call us as when, for example, we are challenged to 'hold firm the confidence and the pride that belong to hope' (Heb. 3.6).

III An ecumenism attentive to the breath of the Spirit

Ecumenical work is also necessary for another very tangible reason. The religious scene has changed dramatically in recent decades, and there has been a significant 'migration' and 'recomposition' within Christendom. In many traditionally 'Christian' countries, especially in Europe, the process of secularization has resulted in a steady decrease in the number of people who call themselves Christians. In contrast, in the global South there has been a significant increase in people identifying themselves as Christians, most notably in Africa, though also in Asia. The number of Christians has grown consistently in the most populous country, China, even though less than 50 years ago the so-called 'cultural revolution' adopted radical measures to discourage any sort of religious belief. In Latin America there has been a striking readjustment within the Christian world, with an impressive growth of Protestant Churches, especially those of a Pentecostal or neo-Pentecostal character, to the detriment of the Catholic community, which was for centuries the official religion of the continent, as a result of its colonization by nations from the Iberian Peninsula.

In numerical terms, Pentecostalism has established itself as one of the great Christian families, alongside Orthodoxy, Catholicism and Protestantism. It shows a striking missionary spirit and an impressive potential to multiply. On the other hand, it is also a movement marked by sharp fragmentation, and is in this sense a reflection in the religious sphere of the cultural fragmentation typical of post-modernity. Thus, after a century of ecumenical endeavour (if we take as our starting-point the

Ecumenical Implications of Reforming the Curia

Edinburgh World Missionary Conference of 1910), the Christian world is more divided than ever. Everything indicates that the so-called 'historic' Churches need to be more attentive to the breath of the Spirit and allow their firmly established structures to move. While it may be true that Pentecostalism could do with a little more institutionality, it is no less true that the historic Churches could do with more mobility.

In view of the points discussed above, one expectation about the reforms in the Catholic Church advocated by Pope Francis is that ecumenism may come to have as prominent a place in the ordinary running of the Catholic Church as it did at Vatican II. Gestures could be very important. A new papal visit to the headquarters of the World Council of Churches in Geneva, for example, would give a clear sign of the importance of ecumenism for the Catholic Church. It would also be very good for the WCC itself and its ecumenical programme. And of course such a gesture would have a great impact in the media and, by no means the least important result, would give new heart to the faithful and the communities in all denominations that are anxious to intensify ecumenical cooperation.

IV   In the service of the people of God:

There are examples to follow and challenges to be faced. In spite of the current state of fragmentation, we do have promising examples of multilateral dialogue and cooperation. In 2011 the World Council of Churches, the Pontifical Council for Interreligious Dialogue and the World Evangelical Alliance produced a joint statement with the title *Christian Witness in a Multi-religious world: Recommendations for Conduct*: this was the first statement in history to represent such a broad range of the Christian family. Recently, an exploratory conversation convened by the Global Christian Forum and held at Bossey in Switzerland recommended that the same dialogue partners, the WCC, the Vatican (the Pontifical Council for Promoting Christian Unity) and the World Evangelical Alliance, with the addition of the Pentecostal World Fellowship, should produce a parallel document, with the suggested title 'Christian Witness in a World of Many Families of Christian Faith: A Guideline for Relations'. The idea of the document is to provide criteria for relations between Churches, especially in situations in which some Churches believe that they are being faithful to their gospel mandate of mission, and others believe that they are being targeted for proselytizing that has no gospel mandate. Achieving a joint statement with this level of broad representativity would be a considerable advance in ecumenism and understanding between the Churches, although the huge task of translating the agreed criteria into church practice on the ground would still remain outstanding.

Obviously, theological dialogues, bilateral and multilateral, should continue. If it has been possible to reach a joint statement about the doctrine of justification, why should it not be possible to move forward on understanding in other areas, for example on ministry? But perhaps even more urgent than new advances in theological dialogues is practical reception of the theological advances already achieved. Wisely, Pope Francis has stressed the need for us to have a keen pastoral sensitivity. This was internal advice for the Catholic Church, but it is valid for all denominations. Jesus Christ, before teaching his disciples, came alongside them in mercy, and not only alongside them, but alongside all who were wounded, excluded and weighed down physically and spiritually.

Couples in mixed marriages (and there are so many) and their families suffer the division between the Churches in a special way. Would it really be theologically objectionable, in view of the progress made in the various dialogues, for eucharistic hospitality to be offered, in particular pastoral situations, between different Christian denominations that agree doctrinally in affirming the real presence of Christ in the Supper? And could that be understood as a first step towards the goal of full eucharistic communion? Could it not be the case that non-theological factors are contributing subliminally, perhaps decisively, a refusal to accept eucharistic hospitality? To be honest, it is important to admit as fact that, in many specific places and situations, the People of God have spontaneously practised such eucharistic hospitality. It would be important pastorally for this to be made possible with due authorization in order not to cause problems of conscience.

I would like to come back to the Second Vatican Council and its amazing feat of *aggiornamento*. Many Protestants, and a great many of the ecumenical observers at the Council, noted with surprise and pleasure many theological and spiritual features very dear to their own tradition. There was, for example, the emphasis placed on Scripture, cherished in the Protestant tradition. And further, there was a move beyond the previous doctrine that divine revelation is divided into two sources, Scripture and tradition, in favour of the recognition that revelation is embodied in Christ himself, the Son of God, come among human beings

Ecumenical Implications of Reforming the Curia

to bring them salvation, and that Scripture and tradition are expressions of this revelation, and not primarily two bodies of doctrine added together. This positive view of tradition (as opposed to the whole range of church traditions), which had already been emerging in ecumenical dialogues involving the Protestant Churches, has led in principle to an abandonment of the dismal centuries-old polemic between Protestants and Catholics over Scripture and tradition.

Protestants also noted with pleasure the liturgical renewal introduced by Vatican II (*Sacrosanctum concilium*), for example the emphasis on Scripture and the homily, and the use of the vernacular in the Mass, measures that had an extraordinary practical impact on communities' devotion, which had been adopted long ago at the beginning of the Protestant Reformation. Liturgical reforms, inspired by ecumenical research, also occurred in the meantime within Protestantism, bringing liturgical celebrations in the different denominations closer together.

Another positive factor for ecumenical relations that I would stress is a series of aspects of the development in ecclesiology initiated by Vatican II, particularly in the Dogmatic Constitution on the Church (*Lumen gentium*): the emphasis on the concept of the People of God and the recognition of the status of local churches. Nevertheless it is true that significant differences still persist in the area of ecclesiology, inevitably because the main obstacles to progress in ecumenism today are to be found in views of the Church. In particular the view taken of the hierarchy in the Catholic Church is markedly different from the conception of the ministerial office of leadership in the Protestant Churches. How far do the differences have to do with the theological conception of ministry or to the way this office is structured in the various Churches? After all, Vatican II, in *Lumen gentium*, also made it very clear that the rôle of the hierarchy must be understood, not as power over the people of God, but as service to it.

V Something deeper than organizational uniformity

In the light of this it seems acceptable and legitimate to consider the appropriateness and need for changes in the way this ministry is exercised and, by extension, in the organizational structure of the Church. The Catholic Church recognizes that there is a 'hierarchy of truths'. Perhaps more radically, the Reformation established a distinction between what is essential and inalienable, on the one hand, and what, while not essential and therefore open to reform, contributes to the well-being of the Church, a distinction expressed in Latin between the *esse* and the *bene esse* of the Church, its being and its well-being.

The Augsburg Confession, drafted by Philipp Melanchthon and approved by Luther, which was presented by the princes who had joined the Reformation to the Emperor Charles V in 1530, became the fundamental profession of faith of the Lutheran Churches. Its aim was to present the Reformed creed as in conformity with the faith of the apostles and the church Fathers, a summary of the Christian faith. Its Article 7 runs: '[The churches, with common consent among us,] teach that one holy Church is to continue for ever. But the Church is the congregation of saints, in which the Gospel is purely preached and the Sacraments rightly administered. And unto the true unity of the Church, it is sufficient [*satis est*] to agree concerning the doctrine of the Gospel and the administration of the Sacraments. Nor is it necessary that human traditions, rites, or ceremonies instituted by men should be alike every where, as St Paul saith: "There is one faith, one baptism, one God and Father of all" [Eph 4.5–6].' Accordingly, the Lutheran Churches have been able to adopt various forms of Church organization, in search of their *bene esse*, without this diversity affecting their unity. Therefore the Churches of the Reformation will certainly be following with interest and watching with sympathy the efforts at reform under way in the Catholic Church. Steps towards decentralization, with an emphasis on collegiality and allowing broad participation in the government of the Church, will be seen as important steps towards the *bene esse* of the Church, and therefore of ecumenical relations.

In the encyclical *Ut unum sint*, Pope John Paul II proposed, setting the example himself, a reflection on the manner in which the papal office itself is exercised. This invitation was certainly genuine and an important initiative, as the Pope saw it. In 1977, when I took part in the Synod of the Americas as president of the Latin American Council of Churches, this was one of the points on which the Pope sounded out the ecumenical representatives, when he honoured us with an invitation to lunch at his residence. For ecumenical relations it is very important to distinguish between the papacy as a symbol of unity and its jurisdictional power, and therefore the more the exercise of the papal office is decentralized, and collegiality in exercising it is affirmed, the closer non-Catholic Christians

Ecumenical Implications of Reforming the Curia

will feel to their Catholic brothers and sisters.

More broadly, this observation also raises the issue of lay participation in decision-making bodies within church government. Although there are different models, in Protestant Churches it is normal and uncontentious for power to be shared between people in ordained ministry and non-ordained members of the People of God. How far will the Catholic Church, in the reform of the Curia, be able to consider the idea of lay participation in decision-making bodies? There can be no doubt that the Protestant Churches will be following possible developments in this area with great interest.

VI *Ecclesia semper reformanda*: an idea we share

In his conversation with journalists during his return flight from World Youth Day in Rio de Janeiro, referring to a possible process of change in the structure of the Catholic Church, Pope Francis used the expression *Ecclesia semper reformanda* ('The Church is always in need of reform'). For the Churches of the Reformation this phrase had a familiar ring, since in their tradition it is attributed to Luther himself. While it is not recorded in that precise form in Luther's writings, it has been mentioned frequently in the Protestant theology of the last 100 years, such as that of the eminent Swiss Reformed theologian Karl Barth. The Lutheran World Federation (LWF) Special Committee Luther 2017: 500 Years of Reformation, in a report approved by the LWF Council, used the expression specifically to stress the Church's need for permanent updating and renewal, as well as the ecumenical (that is, non-exclusive and certainly not triumphalist) dimension that the celebration of the 500th anniversary of the Reformation should have. At the same time it stressed that reforms do not represent any sort of rupture in the Church but that, on the contrary, they should be understood as the return to the apostolic origin of the Church, a process that is permanent, always renewed and essential. The witness of the apostles remains the material criterion for discernment in relation to the change the Church proposes to introduce. This means, therefore, a significant convergence between the Churches.

VII Conclusion

The reform of the Roman Curia that has been announced, while a matter of internal organization that non-Catholics must treat with all respect, whatever the decisions taken, may produce new rapprochements and new opportunities for strengthening ecumenical ties. As such, it is also, indirectly, an important step in the search for church unity, the unity that Jesus bequeathed to his disciples and which he wishes them to preserve or restore today as well.

Translated by Francis McDonagh

Spiritual and Pastoral Guidelines for a Reform of the Roman Curia

PETER HÜNERMANN

I Introduction

There are two basic difficulties in undertaking any such reform: the Church has not integrated essential social and legal developments in its structure, such as the functional separation of legislative, executive and judiciary associated with human rights; and currently the Curia does not represent the Church's basic functions and experience. The requisite reform of the Curia should range from a precise demarcation of essential functions to strictly defined modes of communication and procedure. Unequivocal general principles are needed to create a corporate identity that ensures that the Curia's function and practice accord with the Gospel. These principles should be determined by reference to the Second Vatican Council. The necessary revision of the Curia can succeed only if the appropriate public and specialized debate starts promptly, the requisite initial adjustments are made, and effective strategic measures are taken in good time.

II The situation

The Second Vatican Council was a new approach by the Church to its own and the world's affairs in the midst of a major epochal transformation of humankind. Current discussion among sociologists of culture focuses our attention on three epochal changes in human history that have led to fundamental alterations of the ways in which humans live together, their experience of reality, and how they deal with all aspects of that reality:
1. The sedentarization of human beings, the emergence of agriculture and the associated creation of the first towns in the Neolithic era; 2. the industrialization of the nineteenth and twentieth centuries and a primary transformation of universal knowledge, an understanding of history and

the experience of time, all associated with a major demographic shift; 3. globalization and the emergence of the Anthropocene epoch at the end of the twentieth century and at the beginning of the twenty-first. The term 'Anthropocene' was chosen because humankind has been the most important factor affecting the future of the Earth as a whole in this third great period of transformation. This era is undergoing a scientific and technological shift that allows humans to dismantle reality in its most minute aspects and to reconstruct it, even in new forms and different dimensions that directly affect the nature of life.

At the same time we are experiencing a new diversity in the ways in which personal and social life is structured. This immense increase in the power of disposal and control is based on methodical research oriented to function, specific logical systems, and very extensive controlled chains of action. In the process, a multitude of individual viewpoints is replacing the presumed central perspective on reality that was entirely taken for granted in earlier times. Kant formulated the fundamental philosophical view behind all this and maintained that the possibility of experience constitutively conditions the objects of thought. On the other hand, each object of thought implies the way in which a human being approaches it or the way in which he or she experiences it. This restriction also profoundly affects directly post-Kantian philosophies, such as the phenomenology of Husserl and Heidegger, Wittgenstein's reflections on language, and the methodological assumptions of the natural sciences and the modern humanities.

The Council responded to these emerging changes. They are adumbrated in the introductory chapter of *Gaudium et spes* (The Church in the Modern World), where the conciliar Fathers present the *ratio fidei* (conception of faith) in new terms. This new way of thinking about faith refers back to the approaches of the patristic analysis of faith and the Thomist definition of faith as *virtus infusa* (infused virtue). The Fathers of Vatican II couched their fundamental response in terms of the mystery of revelation (*Dei verbum* [Divine Revelation] 2), the Church (*Lumen gentium* [The Church] 2), the paschal mystery of the liturgy (*Sacrosanctum concilium* [The Sacred Liturgy 2; 5]), and the Kingdom of God (*Gaudium et spes* 40). But they discarded a philosophico-theistic version of the concept of God that arose with Duns Scotus' univocal notion of being and prevailed in various guises from the late Middle

Ages to neoscholasticism.[1] Instead the Council stressed the idea of mystery, of God's plain preconceptuality and the simultaneous fact that human beings are addressed in their freedom yet 'motivated' by God's Spirit: a process which humans are drawn to enter by faith and thereby transcend themselves.

In this way the Council offered something like a programmatic response to the crisis with regard to God in the modern world, which is most apparent in the trend to secularization.[2] It also responded to the emerging church crisis which was palpable in the loss of confidence in a community of faith still intent on combating pre-modern forms of life and their present-day distortions.[3] Both breaking with tradition and communicative dissent are sociologically evident manifestations of the God-crisis *and* the church crisis.[4] To date it has proved possible to carry out only a rudimentary transposition of the highly-complex Vatican II programme into forms of faith and forms of life. The reform of the Roman Curia, the instrument of government and control of the universal Church, is one of the most difficult of the problematical areas to be tackled in this context. Since the structures of the Roman Curia are the institutional reflection of the Petrine ministry of the Bishop of Rome, they profoundly affect not only the understanding and credibility of that ministry, but the understanding and credibility of the whole community of the faithful, the Church.

What kind of reform of the Curia is possible in this context, when the institution to be reformed is not only highly-complex but the object of spiritual and pastoral viewpoints?

I shall try to answer this question by starting from specific difficulties, then describing the challenges to be faced and the spiritual and pastoral guidelines to follow. I shall use the word 'pastoral' in the sense intended by John XXIII and the Fathers of the Council, not with a view to providing immediately practical advice on the everyday exercise of pastoral care based on the application of dogma, but with reference primarily to the Church's self-definition, together with its forms of life and views on life, in modern society as the divinely-empowered witness to the Gospel of Jesus Christ.[5]

I use the word 'spiritual' in the Christian sense to describe the effects, gifts and inspiration of the Holy Spirit moving over chaos from the beginning of creation, as those effects, gifts and inspiration are poured out on the community of the faithful through the risen Lord.

Peter Hünermann

III Basic difficulties and an initial guideline

One primary basic difficulty is that, apart from internationalization, the sole though slight actual changes in the existing structure effected by the reforms of the Curia carried out by Paul VI and John Paul II after the Second Vatican Council were the minimal alterations to the group of nine congregations which both Popes made in conjunction with the Curia itself. The innovations consisted mainly in setting up advisory committees and commissions resulting from the reception of Vatican II. The obvious results were institutional overlaps, and a lack of communication and efficiency.[6]

But the immense changes in human circumstances in the nineteenth century had resulted in a vast number of fundamental social and legal developments to which the Church did not contribute, and which left no trace in its structures. This fact has especially affected the functional separation of legislative, executive and administrative and judiciary. What is at issue here is not a direct adoption of politico-legal constitutional features by and for the Church, but an updating consonant with the nature of the Church or some of its aspects such as a modern form of synodal procedure and a corresponding investigation and implementation of canon law, the introduction of a new balance between the universal Church and local churches, and the primacy and collegiality of bishops, a reconstitution of the judiciary by establishing an administrative jurisdiction, and a new version of the criminal justice system, and so on.

This kind of functional differentiation is essential for the Church. What is in question is the ecclesial transformation of structures which historical experience shows are absolutely essential for the dignity of human existence in modern society. This functional separation represents an evolution and expression of human rights. Here we certainly have to do with an indispensable spiritual and pastoral postulate. It is both spiritual and pastoral because a Church devoid of this differentiation (in its various instances, both as a local church and as a universal Church) would be a body with a sinful 'constitution'. It would be a structure that we could be morally certain would be conducive to numerous social and individual sins. But the Roman Curia needs a new overall concept comprising a clear demarcation of essential functions, unequivocally defined and graduated levels of decision-making, well-organized communication channels, and effectively-regulated procedures. Valuable insights with regard to these qualities are now available from modern economics and the social

Spiritual and Pastoral Guidelines for a Reform of the Roman Curia

sciences, as well as legal studies, and must be taken into account in any reform of the Roman Curia.

A single example will serve to show the complexity of the task now before the Church. The present arrangement of the Curia provides no institution that is responsible for the order of the Church. The Latin church order is taken for granted and there is a congregation for the Eastern churches. It is primarily responsible for the Uniate Eastern Christians, and also sees to contact with the non-Uniate Eastern churches. We also have the recent creation of an 'Anglican Ordinariate', and then we have African, Asian, American but also European churches anxious to express their own cultures and ecclesiastical forms of faith and life. The affirmation of differences of this kind and the manifestation of reciprocal learning processes presume that essential aspects of church order are to be preserved, though in different forms.

This particular complex of problems affects church life at all levels. For instance, in Stuttgart (Germany) alone there are 76 different foreign-language parishes and a considerable number of parishes with their own rites and clergy incardinated in foreign dioceses and in other rites, and subject to the jurisdiction of different bishops.

This example shows how necessary and yet complex the task is. Without a new, duly devised conception of the Curia as a whole, there can be no curial 'order of the Church'. Without it, given the multitude of existing forms of historically-accrued ecclesiastical order, there is no possibility of detecting structural defects in the various church orders and ensuring that they are correctly revised. While acknowledging the plurality of forms of church order, the work of the congregation must include the devising and implementation of certain specific principles of church order to be maintained in different ecclesiastical forms and expressions, such as the abovementioned functional differentiation. We can already begin to discern an initial guideline for ensuring the maintenance of spiritual and pastoral concerns in the reform of the Curia. It concerns the avoidance of structural defects in the new curial structures that have to be provided. Unfortunately the complexity of the situation prohibits even an outline of the major essential aspects of this particular guideline.

We can also detect a second fundamental theological inadequacy of the existing structure of the Curia. At present the Curia does not represent the most basic characteristics of the Church grounded in the tradition of the Church, defined in modern ecclesiology, and expressly confirmed in the texts of Vatican II: *Liturgia* (worship and celebration, prayer and thanksgiving), *Martyria* (witnessing, the proclamation of faith), and *Diakonia* (faith-based activity, works for the poor). Since the Council we have a congregation for divine worship and sacramental order, a certain degree of modernization of the congregation concerned with evangelization of the nations, and, a good 50 years after the Council, a somewhat reinforced papal *Cor unum* advisory body responsible for ecclesiastical charitable institutions.

But these three institutions are not divisions of the Curia directed to essential constitutive principles of the Church. They focus on certain individual aspects of the different operational areas. Therefore the present-day Curia has no possibility of undertaking clear and correct assignments of the various commissions and advisory bodies. Furthermore, the image of the Church as a whole is somewhat awry, since any assignment immediately reveals the position, weighting and task of the different services. At the moment, the basic meaning of *Diakonia*, for example, is not evident.[7]

If the reform of the Curia were to overlook this inadequacy and do nothing to redress it, we might justly speak of a sinfully defective structure, not because human rights would be affected, but because of a lack of respect for the divinely founded nature of the Church.

IV Towards a corporate identity

Deficits in the Church's implementation of basic social and theological developments, which have not been expressed in the structures of the Curia, and are associated with human rights and the essential nature of the Church, are not the only inadequacies which must be taken into account in any reform of the Curia. Another modern development concerns the incorporation of valuable moral aspects in the primary formal structures of control and action systems. Different types of service firms, administrations or industrial producers with socially-relevant, value-oriented, ethical goals have emerged over recent decades. For instance, there are banks with ecological or development-policy business interests, and trading bodies or firms which are concerned about maintaining a duly social or environmentally-aware image, and so on. This development is intimately associated with the abovementioned third 'major transformation'. Advanced scientific research, technology and the media have helped to produce a society that can not only satisfy basic human needs, but (depending on the approach and direction of its research and production and services, and the mechanisms governing the social distribution of goods) fundamentally transform the circumstances of humankind even to the extent of changing the Earth itself. Accordingly, we are now conscious of our manifestly high degree of responsibility for the thrust and direction of all human systems of action if the lived world of human beings is to be opened up for all humans and maintained, especially for future generations.

Starting from the fact that every action and control system comprises a considerable number of decision-makers, and all institutional and functional controls feature scope and leeway for application and execution, these undertakings often devise maxims or watchwords[8] that act as guidelines for action which are incumbent on all concerned in the enterprise, and which determine the decisive mode of application and observation of the system's regulations with reference to its corporate aims. This applies especially to situations in which moral, political, environmentally-relevant, ecological or social interests are pursued or are at least important. These maxims are not only issued, explained and appropriately implemented in the various departments for all those working in the establishment, but are also distributed publicly since they constitute a significant aspect of corporate identity, promote confidence in the services and products on offer, and morally legitimize the acceptance of these services and products by consumers, customers and so on. These maxims or slogans embodying the company's ethos are so to speak the preface to all functional regulations of these firms and organizations.

Many big companies and organizations have some facility within the administration to promote these maxims or some other means of expressing the official philosophy, and to ensure that that the staff are aware of them and observe them in practice.[9]

What does this development have to do with the imminent reform of the Curia, which is one of the most important (if not the most important) of the Catholic Church's systems of action and objectives?

The Second Vatican Council saw itself specifically as locating the Church and its forms of faith and life in the world of our times (*'mundo huius temporis'* [*Gaudium et spes*]), that is, in the universal process of globalization now under way. With regard to this historical movement, the documents of Vatican II have much to say about the innovations to be implemented not only but essentially by the work of the Curia, and by its functional structures.

Even a cursory reference to the individual conciliar documents will immediately reveal a series of innovations from which we can derive a number of salutary maxims or watchwords:

(a) Dignitatis humanae (DH, The Declaration on Religious Liberty) marks a change in the 1,700 years-old tradition of church-state symbiosis, which impaired or prevented religious freedom. This Declaration grounds freedom of religion on human dignity and the radical freedom of belief. *Ad gentes* (*Ad gentes divinitus* [AG, The Decree on the Church's Missionary Activity]) conceives of evangelization and mission accordingly (the appropriate principles appear in *Lumen gentium* [LG, The Dogmatic Constitution on the Church], *Dei verbum* [DV, The Dogmatic Constitution on Divine Revelation], and *Gaudium et spes* [GS, The Pastoral Constitution on the Church in the Modern World]). Consequently: all the Curia's work must serve the freedom of belief by promoting religious liberty, and therefore peace between religions.

(b) Nostra aetate (NA, The Declaration on the Relation of the Church to Non-Christian Religions) ordains the introduction of an essentially dialogal relation with all religions and various groups of non-believers on the basis of God's self-revelation and plan of universal salvation, encompassing the entire history of creation and humankind, and especially the divine covenant with Israel. The four constitutions provide the basis for this decision from different viewpoints.

Consequently: all the Curia's work must serve this comprehensive dialogue.

(c) Gaudium et spes opens up a new form of access to affirming the reciprocally interpenetrative (perichoretic) relation between the modern world and the Church as the sacrament of the Kingdom of God. *Inter mirifica* (IM, The Decree on the Means of Social Communication) belongs in this context. (DV and LG especially provide the basic principles for this viewpoint).

Consequently: all work by the Curia must promote and strengthen this interaction by prudent discernment.

(d) Lumen gentium, but also the other constitutions (*Sacrosanctum concilium* [SC, The Constitution on the Sacred Liturgy], DV, GS), and decrees and declarations such as *Apostolicam actuositatem* (AA, The Decree on the Apostolate of Lay-People), and so on, record the rediscovery of the Church as the people of God, its royal dignity, its priestly and prophetic mission, and its empowerment and competence to effect Christ's Easter mystery. All believers, men and women, are equal in this dignity and mission.

Consequently: Pope and Curia are to serve the people of God, its men and women; they exist for the sake of the people of God, and especially to proclaim the Good News to the poor. The style and work of the Curia must be steeped in this conviction.

(e) Lumen gentium, Orientalium ecclesiarum (OE, The Decree on the Catholic Eastern Churches) and *Unitatis redintegratio* (UR, the Decree on Ecumenism) affirm the fundamental plurality of churches in the Church, which is a plurality according to the interpretation of the apostolic tradition in liturgy, spirituality and theology. This plurality (which increasingly comprises the various local churches of the hitherto relatively uniform 'Latin churches' in Africa, Asia, and South and Central America, but also in North America and Europe, does not aim merely at assembling a number of components but at unity in plurality, characterized by reciprocal recognition and learning from each other.

Consequently: the work of the Curia must be governed by the promotion of this qualitative plurality in all fields.

(f) Lumen gentium, like *Sacrosanctum concilium*, *Christus Dominus* (CD, The Decree on the Pastoral Office of Bishops in the Church), and *Presbyterorum ordinis* (PO, The Decree on the Ministry and Life of Priests), describe the ministry in the Church as service in and for the people of God,[10] so that the whole Church can fulfil its mission. This service in and for the people of God is vested with authority and by virtue of its foundation in Jesus Christ is to be exercised across the entire spectrum of possible forms of collegiality.

Consequently: it may be summarized in the two terms 'ministry (service)' and 'collegiality'.

(g) Lumen gentium and *Unitatis redintegratio* advise us of our duty to

pursue and promote church unity with all our strength and resources. We cannot treat present members of separated churches, and church communities born in those communities, as schismatic sinners. In spite of the absence of unity, the Holy Spirit himself uses these separated churches and communities as means of redemption.

Consequently: the Curia must find time and space among its many tasks to promote and work for ecumenism.

I think that in his brief homilies at morning services for the members of the Curia, Pope Francis tried to emphasize this responsible directedness as desirable in the Curia's various rules of procedure and systems. It is a question of translating the Council's themes and teachings into the Curia as an institutional functional and control system.

V A procedure for reform

The present difficulties of reforming the Curia are not only a matter of its current state. They also largely concern its lack of resources. This lack affects the procedure of choice for reform. The Church lacks a theological and canon-law culture suitable for devising modern forms of ecclesiastical institution. This is because a culture of that kind presupposes the existence of a vital encounter between theology and canon law and developments in the public sphere, such as a constantly renewed development of our own theological and canon-law sources and a universal form of ecclesiastical discourse. Consequently there is a lack of appropriately trained and educated bishops who can act responsibly in these areas, especially since the policy governing episcopal appointments was based essentially on preserving inherited structures. That does not mean that there are no individual bishops with the necessary competences. There are also individual theologians who have published relevant proposals. But there is no such thing as an open form of specialist discourse between canon lawyers and theologians, bishops and theologians, competent experts and public discussion. The lack of any such discourse makes individual publications and occasional statements by individual bishops appear essentially disparate. This absence of dialogue leads to the formation of various dissident groups.

A second difficulty with regard to the process of curial reform which has to be undertaken results from the existing international situation. In response to global human problems, numerous new forms have emerged or are still in the process of institutional formation, in addition to the structures of order tailored to the needs of national States and the corresponding international policy frameworks.[11] The result is an overall precarious *status quo* with various fallow interspaces. Consequently the Church has to face the question of where and how, in respect of the current social situation, the Gospel impels it to take a new direction which calls for appropriate structures in the Roman Curia.[12] In this respect, too, there is a lack of relevant facilities for airing and discussion of the issues involved.

In the first place, then, the process of curial reform possibly calls for a more drawn-out procedure which needs time for a successful outcome.

But longer processes inevitably ask us to confirm the initial measures and decisions that will ensure that the whole endeavour does not collapse prematurely. Are there spiritual and pastoral suasions for choosing a specific introductory approach to an evolutionary process that will (possibly) lead to further self-sustainable developments? There is an unequivocally and clearly affirmative answer to this question. On 6 August 1978, the day when Paul VI died, Giuseppe Dossetti, a theological adviser to Cardinal Lercaro, and together with Lercaro a leading light of the episcopal circle 'Church of the Poor,' stated in a long *Pro memoria* on the change of pontiff, that the first step must be the readiness of the Pope to live the collegiality of the whole Church together with his brother bishops. That was the only way to make sure 'that the primacy is not the arrogance of some worldly power, but the authority of one who is only the first because he is the least of the servants of God (*servorum Dei*), who takes the initiative as Jesus did when he washed the disciples' feet, and serves the cause of the faith of Christians. 'Nothing is so important as the effective exercise of episcopal service in his own Church in a way that banishes the image of the Pope as exerting a bureaucratic power unrelated to faith and to the real problems of his own people'.[13] The most important thing is the creation of a small group of bishops and representatives of the universal Church, analogous to the medieval or early-modern consistory and the synod of the Eastern Churches. It is not primarily a matter of 'monitoring the Curia', as it were, but of ensuring that the Church is administered with the Pope presiding personally in community with the bishops. This announcement, to be made in the course of the first 100 days, would have to involve strengthening the episcopal synod (which was proposed by Vatican II and which Paul VI made the papal consultative body, introducing more frequent meetings and endowing it with legislative powers). That is the

Peter Hünermann

only means by which the different local churches can obtain a greater degree of individual responsibility. It would also be the way to achieve a more effective approach to ecumenical convergence.[14]

Theology and canon law, and prospects of ecclesiastical policy as well as general sociology and organizational psychology, come together here. Dossetti's 'Church of the poor' is an appropriate watchword for an authentic approach to reform of the Roman Curia. It not only covers the spiritual and pastoral dimension of the requisite procedure, but shows that this kind of beginning is the sole way in which we can hope to achieve the sustainable decision to reform the Curia which we can only solicit from God's Spirit. A beginning like this will also free Pope, bishops and associates from the impossible task of having to submit a perfect new order for the Curia starting (so to speak) from nothing.

Translated by J. G. Cumming

Notes

1. *Cf.* Peter Hünermann, 'Continuity and Discontinuity in an Epoch-Making Transition of Faith: The Hermeneutics of Vatican II', a paper given during the conference on 'The Legacy of Vatican II' at Boston College, 26 September 2013.
2. *Cf.* Charles Taylor, A Secular Age, Cambridge, MA, 2007; *id., Philosophical Papers*, 2 vols., Cambridge, MA, 1985; for a discussion of Taylor's thesis see Michael Kühnlein & Matthias-Lutz Bachmann (eds), *Unerfüllte Moderne? Neue Perspektiven auf das Werk von Charles Taylor*, Berlin, 2011.
3. *Cf.* Franz Xaver Kaufmann, *Kirche in der ambivalenten Moderne*, Freiburg im Breisgau, 2012. It is very significant with regard to the complex of problems involved in the reform of the Curia addressed by the present article that a new approach to executive and administrative matters not apparent in the traditional cast of executive and administrative functions became evident directly after the Second Vatican Council. Instead these functions came to be treated on the basis of operating terms and definitions of procedure that were both differentiated yet simultaneously integrated in a context of convergence. *Cf.* Rainer Bucher, 'Neue Machtstrukturen in der alten Gnadenanstalt. Organisationsentwicklung in der Kirche,' in *id.* & Rainer Krockauer (eds), *Macht und Gnade. Untersuchungen zu einem konstitutiven Spannungsfeld der Pastoral*, Münster, 2005, pp. 183–99.
4. *Cf.* F. X. Kaufmann, *op. cit.*, pp. 170–4.
5. I agree with John XXIII's use of the term 'pastoral': 'The reality of the Church in all its dimensions is to be viewed as a pastoral reality.' Quoted by Giuseppe Alberigo in *Transizione epochale. Studi sul Concilio Vaticano II*, Bologna, 2009, p. 40.
6. See the analysis by Thomas von Mitschke-Collande, 'Mentalitätswechsel notwendig. Überlegungen zur Reform der Römischen Kurie', *Herder-Korrespondenz* 67, pp. 443–8, esp. 444f. See also Thomas J. Reese, *Im Inneren des Vatikan. Politik und Organisation der Katholischen Kirche*, Frankfurt am Main, 1998.

Spiritual and Pastoral Guidelines for a Reform of the Roman Curia

7. In his first encyclical Benedict XVI, I am pleased to say, expounded the constitutive significance of this mission of the Church. A certain German bishop declared publicly at around the same time: 'Charity is not an essential concern of the Church.'
8. On the significance of maxims and their varied application in history, see Rüdiger Bubner & Ulrich Dierse, 'Maxime', *HWPh* 5, pp. 941–4.
9. Benedict XVI expressly praised this development in his encyclical *Caritas in veritate* of 29 June 2009 and described it as a major aspect of the overall process of integration (*cf. Caritas in veritate*, esp. Nos 39–42).
10. See also the excellent post-synodal declaration of John Paul II, *Pastores dabo vobis*, 25 March 1992, accessible as: www.vatican.va/holy_father/john_paul_ii/apost_exhortations/documents/hf_jp-ii_ exh_ 25031992_pastores-dabo-vobis_ge.html.
11. Benedict XVI drew attention to a number of these new circumstances in *Caritas in veritate*. See in particular chapters 2–6, pp. 29–117.
12. In this context it is relevant to check whether and how papal committees and advisory bodies set up after the Council should be adapted to these changing situations.
13. Quoted by Giuseppe Alberigo, L'officina bolognese', 1953–2003, Bologna, 2003, esp. p. 209. *Cf.* Peter Hünermann, 'Kirche der Armen. Ein theologisches Programm', *ThQ* 193 (2013/3), pp. 230–41.
14. *Cf., ibid.*

Part Four: Theological Forum

Rio World Youth Day and Evangelization

LÚCIA PEDROSA-PÁDUA

I Introduction

News of World Youth Day (WYD), held only last July in Rio de Janeiro, is still 'hot'. The event demonstrated to the world the popularity of the new Pope in Latin America and among young pilgrims from around the world. It showed the challenges for the Church in its engagement with society and in evangelizing the world of a new generation of young people, in a spirit of unity in diversity. Time, permeated by the Spirit, will give us a more accurate measure of the occasion, but many testimonies describe it as a positive experience that left a mark on the young participants, the Church and even the host city.

II A welcome for the first Latin American Pope

The first point of interest is the warm welcome Pope Francis received on his first journey abroad. Francis's openness to people, welcoming them, conversing with them, touching them and listening to them, his 'normal' person's suitcase (his own words), his call to simplicity as demonstrated in his choice of a modest car, his language, using homely Brazilian phrases to reach out to his audience, his friendly and open manner, all this created a climate of happiness, defused the rejection that was always possible, and ignited new hopes in the Church.

His wish to be among poor communities (the forgotten Varginha *favela*, standing for all Brazil's poor communities) and his call to show that 'things can change', his meeting with disadvantaged young people (drug users and prisoners), displayed solidarity, compassion and warmth.

The Pope's visit to the Marian shrine of Aparecida created reference-points in spirituality (love for Mary) and ecclesiology (the Aparecida document) from the very first. His speeches and homilies to the young people, the poor, the clergy, politicians and civil society were commented on and went down well on the street and in most of the media. His breadth of vision for the Church in Brazil and the rest of Latin America, his positive attitude to CELAM and the bishops' conferences, and his clear call for renewal in the Church provoked enthusiasm, and also put on their guard some who were taken by surprise and preferred to 'correct' the Pope's statements.

The vast majority of Brazilians, including young people, gave the Pope a warm welcome, graphically illustrated by the three and a half million people who came to the final Mass in the dazzling setting of Copacabana beach. For his part, the Pope raised WYD to an unexpected level. It remains to be seen how deep the imprint of this novelty on the Latin American Church and young people will prove to be.

III   A model of evangelization for a new generation

'The memory of the past and the utopia that leads to the future meet in the present'.[1] In terms of history and promise (the implication of the Pope's appeal: 'Let God take you by surprise'), we can think of WYD as a model of evangelization for a new generation of young people culturally globalized, at home in the world of media and technology, less interested in building for the future and searching more for the strong experiences ('adrenalin') that the present has to offer.[2] But at the same time these are young people threatened by massive exclusion from the world of work. Francis's cry to them, 'Don't let yourselves be excluded!', shows his concern at this situation.

WYD is not just a tourist trip, though this dimension was also present in a city like Rio de Janeiro, but a pilgrimage to a meeting with the Pope. The emphatic testimonies of the participants suggest an analogy with the myth of the journey,[3] towards a centre, involving trials but resulting in personal transformation. The centre seduces, radiates meaning, strength for the journey. The trials ensure that the journey leaves a deep mark on pilgrims: they are challenged in their faith and discover the power of solidarity. If post-modern culture claims that centres are unnecessary, we can say that WYD provides a centre for an uncentred world. It creates movement, combines and re-works. In an event full of trials and feeling, it makes reality the metaphor of a generation on a spiritual quest.

Pope Francis was careful to shift the centre of the pilgrimage away from himself and towards Jesus Christ. 'From now on, no more "Francis", but "Jesus",[4] he had insisted to the representatives of the church movements in St Peter's Square in May. During WYD he constantly repeated, in words and actions, the message that the centre is Jesus, who calls us to a mission, especially among the poor.

Francis tried to avoid any impression of 'papolatry', which exists in some more clericalized environments. One sign of the tendency, in some cases, might be the phrase, 'These are the Pope's young people,' repeated incessantly by youth groups. This is an area where the groups need to exercise discernment. Given such discernment, we can say that the meeting with the Pope contains the evangelizing potential to be a pilgrimage for individuals, a generation and a community towards Jesus Christ and his Kingdom.

IV Positives and negatives

Taken as a whole, the Rio WYD was designed to combine mass events with community events, and to include the individual, liturgical, social and cultural dimensions of faith. Five central events (the opening Mass, the welcome for the Pope, the Stations of the Cross, the vigils and the Pope's Mass with the young people) were the visible face of a complex structure, including hundreds of catechesis groups (264 in 32 languages), cultural events and some special events, such as the Pope's activities and meetings with various sectors of the Church and civil society.

Anyone who participated in WYD took away unforgettable experiences. Young people from all over the world transformed the face of the city, with their joy and light-heartedness, and their capacity for sharing, adaptation, goodwill and faith. The meeting events had huge spiritual content. The existential depth of the Stations of the Cross was impressive, and no less moving was the silence of three million people at the vigil: you could hear the sea.

The young people showed generosity in dealing with difficulties like transport, the inadequate provision of portable lavatories on the beach, and even the rain and the cold. For their part, the people of Rio responded on a massive scale with acts of solidarity and hospitality, showing that it possible to break the cycle of fear and violence that keeps many people in big cities imprisoned in their homes.

Lúcia Pedrosa-Pádna

The Pope's relationship with the young people was close and dramatic. He went to the point: following Jesus, faith, solidarity, the capacity for commitment. He was able to get through to the young people, to show that the Church supports them and keeps close to them. He inspired them with a drive to be revolutionary (he used the word), to be able to show commitment in a throw-away world, not to be afraid of happiness, and to be leaders in the search for justice and sharing.

If we look at some of the negatives, we can see how the complex relationship of the Church, with its internal diversity, and the world of politics, civil society, the media, funders and artists, is not free from ambiguities. Political and economic interests and risks were involved.

The most influential media gave good coverage to the main events of WYD and followed every moment of the Pope's time in Brazil. On the other hand, it has to be said that the cultural and ecclesial diversity present in so many WYD events did not always come across. This was the case with the marches against violence and the slaughter of young people, which took place in the days leading up to the main events. They did not attract media interest, even though they expressed one of the main problems of young people in Brazil: violence which is responsible for two-thirds of the juvenile deaths recorded (40 per cent from murder, 20 per cent from traffic accidents and 3.7 per cent from suicide). In 2011 an average of 51 young people were murdered every day.[5] The figures are astounding.[6]

The media images gave huge priority to the celebratory and devotional activities of the young people. The faces of young Christians who work for justice and human rights were hidden.

A particular point needs to be made about the uniformly sugary tone of most of the hymns chosen for several central events of WYD, and in the run-up and sequel. Even the official WYD anthem, which had a different rhythm and called on young people to be missionaries, was rarely played. The impression given was that Catholic young people were almost entirely at one in their liking for gospel music of praise and adoration, characteristic of the movements under Pentecostal and charismatic influence. Is this the only ecclesial and musical style among the young people Pope Francis called on to be 'revolutionary'? My answer to this question would be a clear No.

The use of Latin in the music of the Mass with the young people also surprised many. It was interesting to see that Pope Francis started the Our

Father in his own language (*Padre nuestro...*), but then the microphone was cut to allow the choir to come in with *Pater noster, qui es in caelis...* This decision frustrated those who might have wanted to pray in their own language, along with others who, also in their own languages, would have been reciting the prayer that unites Christians from all parts of the world. As in the Acts of the Apostles (2.6), each person would have understood and been understood, and together they would have spread the awareness that unity and peace are possible within plurality.

V Conclusion

I believe that it is possible to simplify the way huge events like WYD are organized, to ensure better transparency in the relations between Church and society, and to take more care about showing the various faces of the young people. This is not the same as falling into the sterile disappointment that claims that events like this aren't worth the effort, or into the fantasy or arrogance of wanting the wheat without the weeds (Matt. 13.30).

WYD did provide a happy opportunity for hospitality, for communion between different attitudes, for strengthening the 'feeling of faith',[9] and for awakening hope in the Church, with more involvement by young people and the style of the new Pope and support for the internal renewal he is proposing. There were public expressions of approval and welcome for WYD from atheists and people of other Christian denominations and other faiths; this was an exercise in unity in diversity. There was also a firm determination, hard work and even sacrifice on the part of the faithful and pastors of the local church. They took on the responsibility for this event and gave thousands of young people from all over the world a once-in-a-lifetime experience.

We may feel that everyone, and especially the rising generation, deserves to enjoy this heady experience, this 'adrenalin'. Through young people, the Pope said, 'Christ is preparing a new spring throughout the world'. For WYD not to be reduced to a one-off event, the churches have a responsibility to embrace this spring, along with young people, in the everyday follow-up work. May this seed fall on fertile soil, with a good depth and no thorns, and bear fruit.

Translated by Francis McDonagh

Notes

1. The texts of the Pope's various addresses at World Youth Day are available in English on the Vatican website: http://www.vatican.va/holy_father/francesco/travels/2013/papa-francesco-gmg-rio-de-janeiro-2013_en.htm.
2. Cf. the analyses of the 'Generations Y and Z' in J. B. Libanio, 'Juventude e a fé cristã', *Perspectiva Teológica*, Year 45, No. 126 (May/August 2013), pp. 235–66.
3. *Cf.* J. Campbell, *O poder do mito* DVD, Apostrophe S. Productions, 1988.
4. http://www.romereports.com/palio/el-papa-francisco-pide-a-los-movimientos-que-sean-valientes-y-se-dejen-guiar-por-jesus-spanish-10074.html. Accessed on 31 July 2013.
5. J. J. Waiselfisz, *Mapa da Violência 2013. Homicídios e Juventude no Brasil*, Rio de Janeiro, 2013, pp. 16–22.
6. WYD took place near the 20th anniversary of what has become known as the Candelária massacre. In July 1993 police opened fire on children sleeping beside the famous Candelária church in the centre of Rio, killing eight children and young people between the ages of 11 and 19.
7. Over 300 singers took part in WYD, if the cultural events are included. There were Catholic groups, priest singers, and Brazilian and foreign singers. The sociologist Brenda Carranza went so far as to claim that WYD showed the triumph of Catholic gospel music in Brazil. *Cf.* http://www.ihu.unisinos.br/entrevistas/522322-as-intervencoes-do-pontifice-mudaram-de-tom-da-presenca-teologica-para-o-contato-pastoral-entrevista-especial-com-brenda-carranza. Accessed on 2 August 2013.
8. In this aspect, the Mass at the Marian shrine of Aparecida had a very different flavour.
9. The phrase comes from Pedro Poveda, a Spanish priest and founder of the Teresian Association of lay people in 1917.

European Theologians Meet at Brixen, Italy

THIERRY-MARIE COURAU

I Introduction

At the end of August 2013, the bi-annual congress of the European Association of Catholic Theologians (AETC-ESCT) in Brixen-Bressanone (Italy) brought together over 200 theologians, mainly from Europe. They tackled the question of the language that theologians and pastors should use if they wish to be heard and understood, to engage in a constructive dialogue with believers, people seeking enlightenment, and non-believers, and to play a positive role in the social, cultural and political shaping of Europe.

II Changing contexts

The Northern Italian city of Brixen-Bressanone in the South Tyrol (German) or Alto Adige (Italian) region, was formerly home to Bishop Nicholas of Cusa (1401–64). It provided a magnificent backdrop for the meeting of the two assemblies of theologians that followed one another last Summer. From 27 to 29 August 2013, the leading figures of the Regional Assembly of Europe for the Conference of Catholic Theological Institutions (CICT-COCTI) exchanged views on the 'role and challenge of new technologies and the diversity of rationalities in faculties and institutes of theology'. From 29 August to 1 September the bi-annual congress of the European Association of Catholic Theologians (AETC-ESCT[1]) dealt with the theme of 'God in question: religious language and secular language'. This complex of problems, which has concerned theologians for a long time, is still relevant. A group such as the 'Ratzinger Schülerkreis' (the circle of Ratzinger's students), which met at Castel Gandolfo in Summer 2013 (for the first time without Benedict XVI), examined 'the question of God against the background of secularization'. The last bishops' synod and the

Dicastery of the New Evangelization have seen themselves as practical means of resolving this problem.

The search for an answer continues since the relevant contexts are constantly changing. The secularization of societies in the Europe of the past, leaning on an offensive and globalized economic expansion which not only progresses but is deeply entrenched, has as its corollary the rise of religious indifference and an affirmation of non-belief in God, also proposed by people claiming to be Christians. Paradoxically, numerous migratory movements and new ways of life are giving rise to new religious points of view. These are diverse and something of a shock for the religious interests of the world we have lost. Furthermore, the term 'God' is becoming incomprehensible, and even imperceptible, for many contemporaries. In these circumstances, what language should theologians and pastors use to remain heard and understood, to engage in a positive and constructive dialogue with believers, people still searching and non-believers, and for the well-being of the 'social, cultural and political functioning' of Europe'?

III The heart of Europe: centre of gravity

To respond to this question, the organizing committee under the direction of Martin Lintner, OSM, a moral theologian,[2] brought together over 225 theologians from all disciplines and invited 11 researchers, theologians and experts in the human sciences, to participate in five plenary sessions, following an inaugural conference by Bruno Forte, Archbishop of Chieti-Vasto (Italy), on faith and dialogue with non-believers: 1. How does the Bible talk about God? (Arnold Stigmair, Brixen; Ricardo M. Pérez Marques, OSM, Rome). 2. Talk about God as a plea for humanity (Paul Valadier, SJ, Paris; Letizia Ragaglia, Bozen, Director of the Museum of Contemporary Art). 3. Talking about God from experiences of powerlessness (Didier Pollefeyt, Leuven; Tomas Halik, Prague, sociologist).[4] Talking about God in the modern media (Christiane Florin, Bonn, journalist on *Die Zeit;* Stephen Bullivant, London). 5. What is the relationship between the Church and politics in Europe? (Michael Kuhn, Brussels, COMECE [Commission of the Bishops' Conferences of the European Community]; Franz Fischler, former European Commissioner, Austria).

After the plenary sessions, presentations of research, comprising 15 parallel papers and five topics, enabled nearly 60 theologians to participate, largely in German (40 per cent) and in English (40 per cent). The five themed sessions were organized by research centres or laboratories: the Marie-Dominique Chenu Institute (Berlin), the Centre for Ecumenical Research (Leuven), the School of Catholic Theology (Tilburg), the Innsbruck Research Centre and the Anthropos Research Group (Leuven). The panellists' contributions represented very different viewpoints in a secularized and post-modern culture, and helped to deepen and advance the theme of the congress as they questioned the nature of the language used, the relationship between the question of God and that of language, the places of faith, inculturation, dialogue, the arts, and the identity of believers.

The centre of gravity of the meeting of this association, created by Peter Hünermann in 1989, and now with some 800 members (professors, young doctor and doctoral students) from 20 European countries, is at the heart of Europe, with a strong German-speaking presence,[3] and set the tone of the congress.

Two categories of prizes launched the congress. Two authors out of the nine candidates for the prize for the best book on theology for 2011–12 received awards: Leonardo Paris (Trento, Italy) for *Sulla libertà. Prospettive di teologia trinitaria tra neuroscienze e filosofia* (on freedom and trinitarian theology between neuroscience and philosophy), Rome, Città Nuova, 2012, and Michel Younès (Lyons, France) for *Pour une théologie chrétienne des religions* (on a Christian theology of religions), Paris, Desclée de Brouwer, 2012. A competition for the best essay on the congress theme was open to young theologians. The first prize went to Sarah Rosenhauer, a PhD student at the University of Frankfurt am Main (Germany), for an essay entitled *Vom Sinn der Sehnsucht und der Bedeutung des Begehrens. Skizze einer dialektischen Hermeneutik menschlicher Selbstsymbolisierung* (on the meaning of longing and the significance of desire, and towards a dialectical hermeneutics of human self-symbolization). The second prize was given for what was deemed to be a work of equal merit. It went to Daniel Felipe Nino Lopez for *Au-delà d'une question de langage: l'intelligence du christianisme face au monde contemporain* (Beyond a question of language: the mind of Christianity confronted by the contemporary world).

A day before the general assembly, 22 young (doctoral and post-doctoral) researchers presented and discussed their research projects amongst themselves before joining their elders. Their subjects[4] were varied, though mainly grounded in fundamental theology, and offered attempted analyses of Catholic responses to modernity, often in terms of the works of leading authors.

IV Trust and languages

Instead of describing all the authors and the titles and contents of their contributions,[5] I would try to summarize their almost universal thread as something like 'trust as the key to a meeting of languages'. The congress stressed the point that the primary distinction is not one between believers and non-believers, but one between those who 'think' or not, and between those who are looking for the truth or not. Exegetes and biblical scholars try to emphasize, on the one hand, keeping the necessary distance between our contemporary representations of the question of God and biblical symbolic contexts, and, on the other hand, the intensive transformation of biblical and religious language into a sophisticated language serving to legitimize the 'lieutenants of God', to defend doctrine, and even to anathematize those who violate accepted or imposed boundaries.

Nevertheless, the issue of choice of languages, words and signs is of another order: that of allowing hearts to be touched by a living word, to attempt to communicate, and to open a dialogue with the world. It is becoming necessary to listen again to the language of evangelism as the discourse of a God who became human, in relation to this world now, by abandoning any defence of God and his truth at any price. The stress then is on the truth that the evangelization of our contemporaries cannot be thought of as if it were selling some kind of product. Instead it has to be seen as working to reveal their vocation in Christ, which calls for patience and consideration of their various routes and pathways. At a time when European libertarian individualism is distrustful of Catholicism, the churches should be guided by trust in the one who is full of self-doubt rather than fear of a world held to be decadent and corrupt, or a decision to withdraw and fall back on sectarian defensiveness in a counter-culture.

What is required is the witness of Christian life in the sense of accepting all the calls for pastors, too, to trust their people in all the diversity and pluralism of their commitments. Artists also provide a particularly valuable way into our contemporaries' worries and their requests to start from disconcerting, unexpected languages that take the risk of leaving the category of the beautiful in order to plunge into that of the 'terribly human'. Their invocation of religious themes or contexts refers to vital existential situations, which are often as tragic as suffering, exclusion and death can be, and spiritually consonant with the Christ experience. These representations of defeat deploy a totally different aesthetic force which is sometimes shocking and even aggressive, yet no less powerful.

The confrontation of the modern world with evil finds in consideration of the Holocaust an occasion for reformulation and transformation of language faced by the unspeakable. Unlike theological viewpoints that highlight either God's suffering or a radical Manichean form of opposition that gives evil an ontological dimension, the scarcely-invoked theological concept of the absence of goodness can open up interesting prospects, as long as it is complemented by the notion of the perversion of goodness, which is a negative possibility characteristic of all human beings, whoever they are.

Other religious ideas that form part of conventional ecclesiastical discourse, such as glory, sanctity, eternity, resurrection, and so on, though positive, remain inaccessible for many environments, where they arouse perplexity, condescension and even disdain. This lack of understanding on the part of the world can either lead to resentment or arrogance, or even a really hazy conceptualism in Christians, or elicit a cry of joy from recent converts.

What is to be done? What if the ineffective nature of religious language were less a problem of vocabulary than of attitude? Church talk can appear violent and inimical to freedom if too many 'negatives' are heard in public. The negative dimension of ecclesiastical language alienates many people who nevertheless want to come in contact with the Gospel of mercy and intelligence. Specializing as it does in social media, the Church's use of digital technologies is scarcely neutral. It should realize the advantages and risks for its faith, and consider the language that is developing in this sphere. Although these advantages and risks tend to relativize all truth and definitive affiliation and allegiance, they also work as new structures of plausibility that are indispensable for constructing religious identities and for their transmission. It remains to be seen if they will lead those who make use of them to participate in the life of the real world of the Church, and if in this way they will open the way to new horizons of belief with others and to communion between people. We must remember, too, that the future is also the future of Europe. In this respect the representatives of the Churches are not involved at the highest possible levels (see article 17 of the

Treaty on European Union). We have to examine responsibly the tangible investment of the Churches in dialogue with the European Union. Are they merely defending their own interests in so doing, or are they committing themselves to contribute to its fulfilment thanks to their rich traditions?

V Out of the box

The organization of this congress was of an exceptionally high quality and the papers were much appreciated. It enabled an exchange between theologians from important areas of Europe, and different generations of researchers, to take place in a relaxed and confident atmosphere. That is no mean achievement. Nevertheless, the diversity might well have been considerably greater with regard to the geographical origins of the participants, current European trends in theology, and viewpoints. I would like to highlight the absence of perspectives from the new worlds of Africa, Asia, Australasia and the Pacific, and Latin America. The meeting ran the risk of giving the impression that concerns about secularization and evangelization can be resolved by recourse to the knowledge emanating from traditional European ground.

Yet it is obvious that these other continents affect and influence European religious and social experience, whether through migrants, products, companies, political events, or cultural, sapiential and religious traditions. A confrontation with these worlds seemed astonishingly absent from the work of the congress, or as if dialogue with them had taken place for nothing, without effect. But thinking outside the box, travelling in order to open up new perspectives, should be obvious necessities. Of course this has been attempted on the basis of certain non-theological disciplines, but always ad intra rather than ad extra, inside rather than outside the box.

How is it possible to discover the current identity of a European Christian, to ask the question about God and 'talking about God' without meeting these universes, without letting ourselves be disturbed and questioned by other ways of looking at existence, with unknown rationalities,[6] and learning how they live the experience of salvation in Christ? This is certainly the most decisive project that European theologians need to tackle if they want to be able to read and meet a world beyond their immediate grasp.

Translated by Felicity Leng

Notes

1. The Chair for the last two years has been Sigrid Müller, who is head of the theology faculty at the University of Vienna.
2. He teaches at Brixen (Italy) and Innsbruck (Austria). With the 2013 conference he became the new Chair of AETC for the next two years.
3. The heaviest contingents of participants and speakers came from a few Western European countries (Austria, Germany, Benelux and Italy) and represented 50 per cent of participants and speakers. Four Eastern European countries (Hungary, Poland, the Czech Republic and Slovenia) provided 20 per cent of the two categories; and the United Kingdom, Switzerland and Malta 15 per cent (they offered only three papers). Between two and five participants were from North America, Croatia, France, the Republic of Ireland, Lithuania, Portugal, Rumania and Slovakia, and covered less than ten per cent. Four other European countries (Bosnia-Herzegovina, Spain, Estonia and the Ukraine) were represented by one non-participating person. The French, Spanish and Portuguese-speaking worlds were rather poorly represented considering the amount of theology they produce, and the same was relatively true of the primary English-speaking territories.
4. Metaphysics was invoked in regard to church-world dialogue, on the basis of the natural longing for God (Karl Rahner, van Beeck), or the mediating rôle of metaxology [This neologism comes from the complex philosophy of William Desmond, which wrestles with the plurivocity of being. The 'metaxological' stresses the interplay between like and unlike in the ontological matrix of being. TR.]. Commentators on religious or theological language developed their contributions from work on the ethos and practice of the Roman Curia in respect of doctrine, and took into account psychiatry, colonization (Fanon) and the sociology of religion, the life context and spiritual roots of theologians (Dupuis, Haight, Sobrino), the post-modern context, relevant forms of rationality (Gadamer), and the mystery of God and his silence (Newman). Other speakers examined the capacity for dialogue of theological methodology and varieties of theological hermeneutics (Ratzinger, Boeve). Ethical and pastoral contributions addressed such topics as compassion (Aquinas, Nussbaum), the implications of debates on human cryoconservation (cryopreservation) (the Kim Suozzi case), strategies in hospital chaplaincies, and proposed models for pastoral communication and assistance. The list of contributions can be consulted on http://www.hs-itb.it/en/esct-congress-2013-aetc-congres-2013/emerging-scholars-conference-conference-des-jeunes-chercheurs.html.
5. The programme, with details of interventions during the plenary assembly session and topics raised, is accessible at: http://www.hs-itb.it/en/esct-congress-2013-aetc-congres-2013/programme.html.
6. I refer the reader to my article 'The God Question is not Universal', *Concilium*, 2010/4 (September–October: pp. 70–9, and, in general, to that entire issue entitled *Atheists of what God?*).

Contributors

WALTER ALTMANN is a pastor and Lutheran theologian. In 1972 he was awarded a doctorate of the University of Hamburg, Germany, for his thesis on the concept of tradition in the works of Karl Rahner. He was professor of systematic theology in the São Leopoldo/RS theology faculty in Brazil from 1974 to 2002, a post which he has occupied once again since 2011. He was chair of the Latin American Council of Churches (CLAI) from 1995 to 2001, Pastor–President of the Lutheran Evangelical Church of Brazil (IECLB) from 2002 to 2010, and Moderator of the Central Committee of the World Council of Churches (WCC) from 2006 to 2013.

Address: Rua Pastor Rodolfo Saenger, 284
São Leopoldo / RS
BR 93035-110
Brazil
Email: walteraltmann@msn.com

THIERRY-MARIE COURAU OP teaches Buddhism and theology of dialogue at the *Theologicum*, the faculty of theology and religious studies of the Institut catholique de Paris (Catholic University of Paris). He is Dean of the *Theologicum* and president of COCTI, the Conference of Catholic Theological Institutions, a subgroup of IFCU, the International Federation of Catholic Universities. He is a Dominican, and holds a doctorate in Catholic theology of Strasbourg University. He also has diplomas in engineering and management.

Address: Institut Catholique de Paris
21 rue d'Assas
75006 Paris
France
Email: tm.courau@icp.fr

SABINE DEMEL has been professor of church law at the University of Regensburg, Germany, since 1997. Her main research fields are the relation between theology and law, ecumenism, ecclesiastical office, and the legal position of laypeople and women in the Church. Her most recent publications

Contributors

include *Handbuch Kirchenrecht. Grundbegriffe für Studium und Praxis,* Freiburg im Breisgau, second edition 2013; *Frauen und kirchliches Amt. Grundlagen, Grenzen, Möglichkeiten,* Freiburg im Breisgau, 2012.

Address: Lehrstuhl für Kirchenrecht
Universität Regensburg
D- 93040 Regensburg
Germany
Email: sabine.demel@theologie.uni-r.de

MASSIMO FAGGIOLI was a member of the Pope John XXIII Foundation in Bologna from 1996 to 2008. He teaches the history of Christianity at the University of St Thomas, Minneapolis/St Paul (USA). His pubished works include: *Il vescovo e il concilio. Modello episcopale e aggiornamento al Vaticano II* (2005); *Breve storia dei movimenti cattolici* (2008; Spanish translation 2011, English translation forthcoming); *Vatican II: The Battle for Meaning* (2012; Italian and Portuguese translations 2013); *True Reform: Liturgy and Ecclesiology in Sacrosanctum Concilium* (2012; Italian translation 2013); *Nello spirito del concilio. Movimenti ecclesiali e recezione del Vaticano II* (2013).

Address: University of St. Thomas
Department of Theology – JRC 153
2115 Summit Avenue
St Paul, MN 55105
USA
Email: massimo.faggioli@gmail.com

PETER HÜNERMANN was born in Berlin in 1929. He read philosophy and theology in Rome, Munich and Freiburg im Breisgau, Germany, and holds several doctorates. He was ordained a priest in 1955. From 1971 until his retirement he was professor of dogmatic theology, first in Münster, and then in Tübingen from 1982. His publications include *Jesus Christus – Gottes Wort in der Zeit* (1994); *Ekklesiologie im Präsens* (1995); *Papstamt und Petrusdienst: ein dringliches innerkirchliches und ökumenisches Problem* (1998); *Herders Theologischer Kommentar zum Zweiten Vatikanischen Konzil* (editor with B. J. Hilberath, 5 vols, 2009). His last article for *Concilium* was 'Speechless about Vatican II?' in the 2012/3 issue.

Contributors

Address: Engwiesenstr. 14
72108 Rottenburg a. N.
Germany
Email: peter.huenermann@uni-tuebingen.de

HERVÉ LEGRAND OP was born in 1935 at Quimper (France). He studied in the Dominican Saulchoir faculty, and at the universities of Bonn, Strasbourg, Rome (St Thomas Aquinas) and Athens. He is a specialist in ecclesiology and honorary professor in the theology faculty, Paris, where he directed the Higher Institute of Ecumenical Studies and the supervision of doctoral theses. He is an adviser to the European Council of Bishops' Conferences and a member of several ecumenical dialogue commissions, especially with the World Lutheran Federation. He is currently vice-chair of the International Academy of Religious Science.

Address: 20, rue des Tanneries
F-75013 Paris
France
Email: hervelegrandop@yahoo.fr

GERARD MANNION holds the Amaturo Chair in Catholic Studies and is Fellow of the Berkeley Centre for Religion, Peace and World Affairs at Georgetown University. Educated at the Universities of Cambridge and Oxford, he has previously worked in Britain (Oxford, Leeds, Liverpool), Leuven (Belgium) and San Diego. He is an honorary Fellow of the Australian Catholic University and has held visiting professorships and fellowships at Tübingen (Germany), Chichester (England) and the Institute of Religious Sciences, Trento (Italy). He is founding chair of the Ecclesiological Investigations International Research Network, and editor of its book series. He has published widely in the fields of ecclesiology, ethics and other aspects of systematic theology and philosophy. He is an Irish citizen, and passionate about social justice, rugby union and music.

Address: Department of Theology
Georgetown University
Box 571135, New North 102
Washington, DC 20057-1135

Contributors

USA

ALBERTO MELLONI was born in Reggio Emilia, Italy, in 1959. He is professor of the history of Christianity at the University of Modena/ Reggio and director of the foundation for religious science. He edited the Italian edition of the S*toria del concilio Vaticano II*, Bologna, 1995–2001; his publications include: *Papa Giovanni. Un cristiano e il suo concilio* (Einaudi), *Tutto e niente. I cristiani d'Italia alla prova della storia* (Laterza) and *Quel che resta di Dio. Un discorso storico sulle forme della vita cristiana* (Einaudi). He was general editor of the *Enciclopedia Costantiniana* in three volumes and the author of *Il conclave di papa Francesco*.

Address: Via Università 4
41121 Modena
Italy
Email: alberto.melloni@tin.it

LÚCIA PEDROSA-PÁDUA is professor of theology at the PUC-Rio (Brasil), and specializes in anthropology, mysticism and spirituality. He studied theology at the Jesuit FAJE faculty at Belo Horizonte (Brazil) and holds a doctorate from the PUC-Rio. He also holds a degree in economics from the UFMG. He is a member of the permanent assessors' commission of the CNLB. He is director of studies at the Ataendi Centre of Teresian Spirituality and the author of various publications in the fields of anthropology and mysticism.

Address: Rua Jardim Botanico 616/504-A
22461-Rio de Janeiro RJ
Brazil
Email: lpedrosa@puc-rio.br

DOM CELSO QUEIROZ was auxiliary Bishop of São Paulo from 1976 to 2000. He was part of a college of ten bishops alongside Cardinal Paulo Evaristo Arns that governed the city of São Paulo, in which each bishop headed a relatively autonomous area. When the Holy See divided the archdiocese into autonomous dioceses, he became bishop of Catanduva, in the north-west of the State of São Paulo. He was an adviser, secretary general and vice-president of the Brazilian bishops' conference from the 1970s to 2003.

Contributors

He worked in the Brazilian National Council of Christian Churches. Today he is a lecturer and retreat-giver.

Address: Rua Guararema, 707 – apto 101.
04136-031
São Paulo – SP
Brazil
Email: Domcelso33@bol.com.br

THOMAS J. REESE SJ is a senior analyst at the *National Catholic Reporter* (NCRonline.org) and author of *Inside the Vatican: The Politics and Organization of the Catholic Church* (Harvard University Press, 1996). He was a senior fellow at the Woodstock Theological Center at Georgetown University (1985–98, 2006–13), where he used his political science training (PhD, University of California Berkeley) to examine the Catholic Church. He was editor-in-chief (1998–2005) and associate editor (1978–85) at *America* (americamagazine.org).

Address: 1726 New Hampshire Ave NW
Washington, DC 20009-2526
USA
Email: treese@NCRonline.org

NORMAN TANNER SJ is professor of church history at the Gregorian University, Rome. Born in Britain, he entered the Society of Jesus aged 18 in 1961 and was ordained a priest in 1976. For many years he taught in the history and theology faculties at Oxford University, while also giving short courses on church history and councils in many countries. He moved to Rome in 2003. His publications include: *Decrees of the Ecumenical Councils* (2 vols, 1990); *The Councils of the Church: A Short History* (2001), translated into Italian, French, Spanish, Indonesian, Japanese and Korean; *New Short History of the Catholic Church* (2011), available on 'Kindle' and translated into various languages.

Address: Piazza della Pilotta, 4
00187 Rome
Italy
Email: tanner@unigre.it

CONCILIUM
International Journal of Theology

FOUNDERS
Anton van den Boogaard; Paul Brand; Yves Congar, OP; Hans Küng; Johann Baptist Metz; Karl Rahner, SJ; Edward Schillebeeckx

BOARD OF DIRECTORS
President: Felix Wilfred
Vice Presidents: Thierry-Marie Courau; Diego Irarrázaval; Susan Ross

BOARD OF EDITORS
Regina Ammicht Quinn (Frankfurt, Germany)
Mile Babić (Sarajevo, Bosnia-Herzogovina)
Maria Clara Bingemer (Rio de Janeiro, Brazil)
Erik Borgman (Nijmegen, The Netherlands)
Lisa Sowle Cahill (Boston, USA)
Frère Thierry Marie Courau (France, Paris)
Hille Haker (Frankfurt, Germany)
Diego Irarrázaval (Santiago, Chile)
Solange Lefebvre (Montreal, Canada)
Eloi Messi Metogo (Yaounde, Cameroon)
Sarojini Nadar (Durban, South Africa)
Daniel Franklin Pilario (Quezon City, Philippines)
Susan Ross (Chicago, USA)
Silvia Scatena (Reggio Emilia, Italy)
Jon Sobrino SJ (San Salvador, El Salvador)
Luiz Carlos Susin (Porto Alegre, Brazil)
Andres Torres Queiruga (Santiago de Compostela, Spain)
João J. Viba-Chã (Portugal)
Marie-Theres Wacker (Münster, Germany)
Felix Wilfred (Madras, India)

PUBLISHERS
SCM Press (London, UK)
Matthias-Grünewald Verlag (Ostfildern, Germany)
Editrice Queriniana (Brescia, Italy)
Editorial Verbo Divino (Estella, Spain)
EditoraVozes (Petropolis, Brazil)
Ex Libris and Synopsis (Rijeka, Croatia)

Concilium Secretariat:
Asian Centre for Cross-Cultural Studies,
40/6A, Panayur Kuppam Road, Sholinganallur Post, Panayur, Madras 600119, India.
Phone: +91- 44 24530682 Fax: +91- 44 24530443
E-mail: Concilium.madras@gmail.com
Managing Secretary: Arokia Mary Anthonidas

Concilium Subscription Information

February 2013/1: *Reconciliation: Empowering Grace*

April 2013/2: *Postcolonial Theology*

August 2013/3: *Saints and Sanctity Today*

October 2013/4: *The Ambivalence of Sacrifice*

December 2013/5: *Rerforming the Curia*

New subscribers: to receive *Concilium 2013* (five issues) anywhere in the world, please copy this form, complete it in block capitals and send it with your payment to the address below.

Please enter my subscription for *Concilium 2013*

Individuals
____ £50 UK
____ £72 overseas and Eire
____ $95 North America/Rest of World
____ €85 Europe

Institutions
____ £72 UK
____ £92 overseas and Eire
____ $110 North America/Rest of World
____ €135 Europe

Postage included – airmail for overseas subscribers

Payment Details:
Payment must accompany all orders and can be made by cheque or credit card
I enclose a cheque for £/$/€ ____ Payable to Hymns Ancient and Modern Ltd
Please charge my Visa/MasterCard (Delete as appropriate) for £/$/€ ____

Credit card number _____

Expiry date _____

Signature of cardholder_____

Name on card _____

Telephone _____E-mail _____

Send your order to *Concilium*, **Hymns Ancient and Modern Ltd**
13a Hellesdon Park Road, Norwich NR6 5DR, UK
E-mail: concilium@hymnsam.co.uk
or order online at www.conciliumjournal.co.uk

Customer service information
All orders must be prepaid. Subscriptions are entered on an annual basis (i.e. January to December). No refunds on subscriptions will be made after the first issue of the Journal has been despatched. If you have any queries or require information about other payment methods, please contact our Customer Services department.

MAKING OUR CONNECTIONS
A SPIRITUALITY OF TRAVEL
PINK DANDELION

We can now travel more than we ever could before. Indeed, travel is now part of everyday life for most of us, whether to or for work, or on holiday - but how do we enhance our spiritual lives as we constantly head off to somewhere else.

Here is a book about the everyday, reflecting on all kinds of travel. Pink Dandelion offers directions we may take to reclaim and rediscover an attitude to travel that builds community, and through that enhance our sense of Spirit at work in our lives and in the world.

9780334044086 • Paperback • £19.99

ORDER DIRECT FROM SCM PRESS

Website: www.scmpress.co.uk
Tel: 01603 785 925
E-mail: orders@norwichbooksandmusic.co.uk
Also available from all good Christian bookshops.

www.ingramcontent.com/pod-product-compliance
Lightning Source LLC
Chambersburg PA
CBHW051402290426
44108CB00015B/2128